THE DECREES OF THE DEMOTIONIDAI

American Philological Association
American Classical Studies

The Harmonics of Nicomachus and the Pythagorean Tradition	Flora R. Levin
The Etymology and the Usage of ΠΕΙΡΑΡ in Early Greek Poetry	Ann L. T. Bergren
Two Studies in Roman Nomenclature	D.R. Shackleton Bailey
The Latin Particle Quidem	J. Solodow
On the Hymn to Zeus in Aeschylus' Agamemnon	Peter M. Smith
The Andromache of Euripides	Paul David Kovacs
A Commentary on the Vita Hadriani in the Historia Augusta	Herbert W. Benario
Creation and Salvation in Ancient Orphism	Larry J. Alderink
Eros Sophistes: Ancient Novelists at Play	Graham Anderson
Ancient Philosophy and Grammar: The Syntax of Apollonius Dyscolus	David Blank
Autonomia: Its Genesis and Early History	Martin Ostwald
Language and Metre: Resolution, Porson's Bridge, and Their Prosodic Basis	A. M. Devine
Descent from Heaven: Images of Dew in Greek Poetry and Religion	Deborah Boedeker
Iamblichus and the Theory of the Vehicle of the Soul	John F. Finamore
Epicurus on the Swerve and Voluntary Action	Walter G. Englert
Seneca's Anapaests	John G. Fitch
Xoana and the Origins of Greek Sculpture	A. A. Donohue
ANAΓKH in Thucydides	Martin Ostwald
Old Comedy and the Iambographic Tadition	Ralph M. Rosen
EKΩN and AKΩN in Early Greek Thought	GailAnn Rickert
Hekate Soteira	Sarah Iles Johnston
The Decrees of the Demotionidai	Charles W. Hedrick, Jr.

Charles W. Hedrick, Jr.

THE DECREES
OF THE DEMOTIONIDAI

Scholars Press
Atlanta, Georgia

THE DECREES OF THE DEMOTIONIDAI

Charles W. Hedrick, Jr.

© 1990
The American Philological Association

Library of Congress Cataloging in Publication Data

Hedrick, Charles W.
    The decrees of the Demotionidai / Charles W. Hedrick, Jr.
    p. cm. -- (American classical studies ; no. 22)
    Includes bibliographical references and index.
    ISBN 1-55540-466-9 (alk. paper). -- ISBN 1-55540-467-7 (pbk. :
    alk. paper)
    1. Inscriptions, Greek--Greece--Attikē. 2. Attikē (Greece-
Antiquities. I. Title. II. Series.
CN373.H43 1990
938'.5--dc20   90-47456
                                                     CIP

Printed in the United States of America
on acid-free paper

TABLE OF CONTENTS

Preface		vii
Chapter One	History of the Inscription	1
Chapter Two	Text and Translation	5
	Bibliography	6
	Text	7
	App. Crit.	10
	Epigraphical Notes	11
	Translation	14
Chapter Three	General Commentary	19
	Organization of the Inscription	19
	Section 1: the Heading	20
	Section 2: Erection of the Stele	21
	Section 3: the Priestly Perquisites	25
	Section 4: the Preamble	30
	Section 5: the Decree of Hierokles	33
	Section 6: the Decree of Nikodemos	55
	Section 7: the Decree of Menexenos	59
Chapter Four	The Scrutinies	61
	Introduction	61
	Procedure of the "Extraordinary" Scrutiny	61
	The "Regular" Scrutiny	68
	The "Regular" and "Extraordinary" Scrutinies	72
Chapter Five	The Demotionidai and the House of the Dekeleians	75
	Introduction	75
	Thiasos, Phrateres and Demotionidai	78
	House of the Dekeleians	80
Bibliography		87
	Abbreviations	87
	Works Cited	89
Indices		95
	Index to the Inscription	95
	Index of Modern Authors	98
	Index Locorum	100
	Index of Selected Greek Words	104
	General Index	106
Illustrations		111

The phratry is attested throughout the Ionian city-states. Other analogous institutions are known among the Dorians and Aeolians. Typically, though, the evidence for such organizations in most parts of the Greek world is extremely sketchy. The phratry is most extensively documented in Attica; in fact, the evidence for the Attic phratry has necessarily served as the basis for modern generalizations about similar institutions elsewhere in the Greek world.

The phratry was surely one of the most important social and political institutions of the ancient Athenian state. Because the group was charged with the arbitration of many male (and some female) "rites of passage," it ultimately determined the articulation of social status among citizens and guaranteed the standards of citizenship. The phratry was also a pervasive presence in the social and religious life of the community. Its role in the various Attic festivals, such as the Thargelia, Anthesteria, Greater Dionysia, Synoikia and, above all, the Apatouria, is well known.

Despite its evident importance, contemporary references to the phratry, even in Attica, are relatively few and surprisingly casual. Only three formal, general essays dealt with the group, even tangentially. None of these has survived complete.[1] Beyond these lost works, the phratry evidently did not attract the attention of ancient scholars. Even the Atthidographers, who might have been expected to discuss the institution, are silent.[2] In the absence of any extant ancient general account, it is necessary to rely on the incidental literary references to the group, especially those of the orators, and the

---

[1] The lost beginning of the Aristotelian *Constitution of Athens* included a description of the phratry in its pages on the early Athenian state. See *AP*, F. 5 Opp. with the remarks of Rhodes, *A Commentary on the Aristotelian Athenaion Politeia*, Oxford 1981, pp. 68-71. Demetrius of Phaleron also very likely discussed the phratry in his lost essay on the Athenian Constitutions: for Demetrius and his writings see *FGrHist* 228. Dikaiarchos, the fourth century Peripatetic, also seems to have written on phratries in his cultural history of Greece, the Βίος Ἑλλάδος: see F. Wehrli, *Die Schule des Aristoteles* I, Basel 1944, F. 52 = Steph. Byz. *s.v.* πάτρα; M. Guarducci, "L'istituzione della fratria nella Grecia antica e nelle colonie greche di Italia," parte prima, *MAL* ser. 6, 6 (1937), pp. 6-7.

[2] The Atthidographers only provide information in cases where the phratry is linked with the great figures of the Athenian tradition, in particular Ion, Solon and Kleisthenes. See F. Jacoby, *Atthis: the Local Chronicles of Ancient Athens*, Oxford 1949, p. 316 n. 40; *idem*, commentary to *FGrHist* 328 (Philochoros), F. 94, p. 395 and n. 31; F. 35, p. 321.

specific, though laconic testimony of the inscriptions.[3] Finally, there is the equally contingent but less reliable information provided by the later scholiasts and lexicographers.

Indisputably the single most enlightening document dealing with the Attic phratry is the "Inscription of the Demotionidai," *IG* II[2] 1237. This inscription provides a dossier of three phratry-decrees, inscribed on a single stele over a period of 40 years, from 396/5 to the 360's. All three of the decrees concern the procedures which govern admission to the phratry. These decrees provide incidental information about the internal organization of the phratry, as well as its relationship to other groups. They constitute the fullest documentation by far pertaining to any individual Attic phratry.

The text of this inscription has been intensively studied since the turn of the century. A huge bibliography has accumulated concerning every aspect of the decrees: they are discussed in all histories of the Athenian constitution, as well as in most general accounts of Greek history, society and political antiquities. Individual studies devoted to the inscription have proliferated. It may be helpful, then, at the outset to provide reasons which justify a new edition and commentary.

The "Inscription of the Demotionidai" was discovered on the summer estate of the King of Greece at Tatoi, where it has been preserved in isolation. Because of this accident of provenience, it has never been easily available to scholars. From the time of its discovery, virtually all editions of the text have been based on squeezes. There has never been a detailed description of the stone; only two photographs of it have been published, both in an obscure volume, long out of print, by the princesses, Sophia and Eirene, and the royal tutor, Theophano Arvanitopoulou. No thorough description of the physical text has ever been published.[4]

Though the edition of the text provided here has resulted in only one new reading, the accompanying description of the text is, in itself, an important addition to the bibliography. The new information concerning erasures and variations in the *stoichedon* pattern which has emerged dictates considerable modification to the currently accepted interpretation of the text. In addition, I provide for the first time accessible and detailed photographs of the stone.

---

[3] For a catalogue of the literary and epigraphical references to *specific* Attic phratries see C. W. Hedrick, Jr., "The Phratry Shrines of Attica and Athens," *Hesperia*, forthcoming.

[4] An account of the history and bibliography of the inscription since its discovery is provided in Chapter One.

There have been no full commentaries on this document since the beginning of the twentieth century.[5] A contemporary commentary is needed. The language of these decrees is not easily comprehensible. It is by turns technical and idiosyncratic, and has often been incorrectly understood, even by specialists. In the third chapter I provide a general commentary on the text, with discussion of difficult passages and a synopsis of the bibliography. Unless an issue is controversial I have been brief, providing only summary explanation and essential bibliography.

The final chapters of this study are devoted to a new interpretation of the most notorious problems associated with this document. In the fourth chapter I re-examine the procedure of the "extraordinary" διαδικασία and evaluate its relationship to the "regular" διαδικασία. In the fifth chapter I attempt to identify the Demotionidai and the House of the Dekeleians.

I began my work on the Demotionidai with a term paper for a class given by Martin Ostwald on the Aristotelian *Constitution of Athens*. This paper developed into my doctoral dissertation.[6] I should like to acknowledge here the help and encouragement of Professor Ostwald, as well as that of the other members of my dissertation committee: Professor A. John Graham and Professor Robert E.A. Palmer.

I have had the benefit of benevolent criticism from many quarters. Professor Michael Jameson and Dr. David Lewis read an early draft of my arguments and kindly contributed their comments. Jack Peradotto has aided and abetted my work in ways too manifold to enumerate. Madeleine Kaufman helped with the thankless job of proofreading this difficult manuscript. I have profited from correspondence with Stephen Lambert. In particular, it is a pleasure to acknowledge a debt incurred in many hours of conversation and argument with Josh Ober.

My research on the decrees of the Demotionidai has obviously benefited from the opportunity to examine the inscription in person. A grant from the Fulbright Foundation made it possible for me to spend a uninterrupted year on my research in Greece. The American School of Classical Studies in Athens extended me its usual generous hospitality, as well as the use of its library.

---

[5] See, *e.g.*, *RIJG* II, no. 29 pp. 199-227, and, most recently, F. Hiller von Gärtringen in *SIG*[3], no. 921. Recent studies have focused narrowly on the first of the three decrees, and more specifically on the problem of the relationship between the Demotionidai and the House of the Dekeleians.

[6] *The Attic Phratry* (Thesis, University of Pennsylvania), Ann Arbor 1984.

Many scholars in Greece aided me in my endeavors to locate the inscription of the Demotionidai. In particular I would like to single out Judith Binder, John Camp, Stephen Miller, Dina Peppas-Delmousou, Gerhardt Schmidt and Eugene Vanderpool. In particular I must acknowledge the aid of Markellos Mitsos, who took an almost personal interest in locating the inscription. The Secretary of the American School in Athens at the time, Murray McClellan, obtained necessary permits for me. Finally, I thank the archivists of the photograph collection of the *Deutsches Archäologisches Institut* in Athens, who dispatched a member of their staff to the Royal Estate to photograph the inscription for me.

I could not have gained access to the Royal Estate at Tatoi without the permission of the Greek agencies responsible for it: the Second *Ephoria* of the Greek Archaeological Service, which is responsible for the antiquities of that region, and the Ministry of Agriculture, which is in charge of the physical plant of the estate. The caretaker of the estate, Mr. Lellingos, was helpful and friendly. Above all I must thank the manager of the royal estates in Greece, the Ναύαρχος Stavrides. Without his willing cooperation I could never have seen the inscription.

Successive Chairs of the APA Editorial Board for Monographs, Professor Ludwig Könen and Professor Matthew Santirocco, have supervised the passage of this essay from manuscript to book. Along the way the remarks of anonymous readers have materially improved and sharpened the substance and presentation of my ideas. The Julian Park Foundation has defrayed some of the costs of publishing glossy photographs of the inscription.

I dedicate this monograph to my wife, Charmaine Curtis, who tolerates and even occasionally encourages my impractical and unremunerative obsession with things Greek.

August, 1990
Santa Cruz, California

CHAPTER ONE

HISTORY OF THE INSCRIPTION

An account of the discovery of the inscription recording the "decrees of the Demotionidai" and of its subsequent history will be important for an understanding of the development of the modern interpretations of the documents. The account will also be of some intrinsic interest to those who are concerned with the antiquities of Dekeleia.

In 1883 the director of the Royal Estate at Tatoi, L. Münter, undertook excavations in the vicinity of the stables of the King of Greece. The area, known locally as Μεγάλη Βρύσις or "Great Spring," lies on the ancient road from Dekeleia to Acharnai.[1] The inscription of the Demotionidai was discovered in a wall during these excavations. It was then moved to the "living-room of the Director of the Estate," which was to be its home for the next seventy years.

Münter did not initially realize that both sides of the *stele* were inscribed: face B could not be read because it was caked in cement. So, on the fifteenth of May, 1883, he sent a transcript of face A only to S. Koumanoudes. Three days later he provided that same scholar with a squeeze. Koumanoudes then published the *editio princeps* of face A, submitting it to the Άρχαιολογικὴ Έφημερίς on the twenty-ninth of May.[2] That same year U. Köhler also edited face A of the inscription for the first edition of the *Inscriptiones Graecae*. Köhler, like Koumanoudes, did not see the inscription. He based his text on a squeeze "provided by Lolling."

In the summer of 1888, Münter had the back of the *stele* cleaned and discovered that it too was inscribed. He quickly sent a copy and squeeze of the new text to J. Pantazides, who published the *editio princeps* of face B in a local newspaper (cited only by the generic title, "the Έφημερίς") of September 1-13, 1888.[3] H. Lolling, using the text provided in this newspaper

---

[1] See S. Koumanoudes, "Ψήφισμα Φρατερικόν," *ArchEph* (1883), cols. 69-70, and H. Lolling, " Άνασκαφαὶ καὶ εὑρήματα ἐν Δεκελείᾳ," *AD* 4 (1888), pp. 159-160. A map (unnumbered) is provided in Th. Arvanitopoulou, with Sophia and Eirene, Princesses of Greece, Όστρακα ἐκ Δεκελείας, Athens 1959.

[2] S. Koumanoudes, "Ψήφισμα Φρατερικόν," *ArchEph* (1883), cols. 69-76.

[3] I have not been able to locate a copy of this newspaper article. For its contents, see H. Lolling, " Άνασκαφαὶ καὶ εὑρήματα ἐν Δεκελείᾳ," *AD* 4 (1888), p. 160.

article, re-edited the text in the ' Αρχαιολογικὸν Δελτίον of 1888.[4] Meanwhile Pantazides produced the first complete edition of faces A and B, which he submitted to the 'Αρχαιολογικὴ 'Εφημερίς on the fifteenth of September, 1888.[5] There is no indication that any scholar had access to the inscription for the next seventy years. Virtually all modern texts are based on these early publications, none of which are themselves based on autopsy of the stone.

The decrees were edited for the first and only time from autopsy in 1958 by Theophano Arvanitopoulou.[6] Though this publication makes no improvement over previous editions of the text, it has the great virtue of including photographs of squeezes of the text. The following year, the Princesses Sophia and Eirene, with Arvanitopoulou, published photographs of the stone itself. The book in which the photographs were published[7] was issued to illustrate the collection of the "Museum of King George I." According to Arvanitopoulou, the inscription of the Demotionidai was to be part of this collection.

The "Museum of George I," sometimes called "the Pyrgos" by nineteenth-century scholars, was destroyed in the fire which devastated a large part of the estate in 1916.[8] The museum and its contents lay in ruins until 1958, when the two princesses of Greece, Sophia and Eirene, and their tutor, Theophano Arvanitopoulou, excavated it to recover the antiquities which lay in its rubble.[9]

According to Arvanitopoulou's account, after they cleared the floor of the museum, they cleaned the antiquities which they discovered there and placed them "in the museum." They also added to the collection the antiquities found in their own excavations on the estate. At this time they also "removed the inscription of the Demotionidai from the office of the manager of the estate." They note, however, that they did not place anything in the museum which might be destroyed by the elements, for the museum was "not

---

[4] *Ibid.*, pp. 159-163.

[5] J. Pantazides, " 'Επιγραφὴ ἐκ Δεκελείας," *ArchEph* (1888), cols. 1-20.

[6] Th. Arvanitopoulou, Δεκελεία (Πολέμων, παράρτημα), Athens 1958.

[7] Th. Arvanitopoulou, with Sophia and Eirene, Princesses of Greece, "Οστρακα ἐκ Δεκελείας, Athens 1959, εἰκ. 14-15.

[8] Generally for the history of the museum, see F. Willemsen, "Vom Grabbezirk des Nikodemos in Dekeleia," *MDAI(A)* 89 (1974), p. 176.

[9] Th. Arvanitopoulou, with Sophia and Eirene, Princesses of Greece, "Οστρακα ἐκ Δεκελείας, Athens 1959, p. 9.

yet" roofed.[10] The museum was never roofed: in their book the princesses and Arvanitopoulou provide a photograph of the museum with the collection *in situ*, as they left it:[11] their "museum" was an open, unwalled floor in the middle of a pine forest. In the summer of 1983 I examined the museum: it, and the antiquities "in" it were undisturbed. Everything visible in the 1959 photograph was exactly in place, but the inscription of the Demotionidai was not to be found, nor were any of the more valuable pieces known to be at Tatoi.[12] Clearly the most precious objects of the collection were never placed in the museum, in spite of the account given by Arvanitopoulou, but were preserved in some sheltered place.

When Constantine II fled Greece in 1967, the estate at Tatoi was closed. His possessions in Greece nevertheless remained his personal property; the royal collection of antiquities was not confiscated at this time but was locked up with the estate.

In 1983, after examining the "Museum of George I," I approached the manager of the royal estates in Greece, the Ναύαρχος Stavrides, and asked his help in locating the inscription. He kindly promised to check in "two or three likely places." He located the inscription in an ἀποθήκη "where the royal family kept objects not currently in use." The Ναύαρχος removed the inscription from this store room to the house of the caretaker of the Estate, where I was able to study it and take squeezes. At this time members of the Deutsches Archäologisches Institut photographed it for me. The Ναύαρχος Stavrides then replaced the inscription in the store room where he had found it.

---

[10] *Ibid.*, p. 12.

[11] *Ibid.*, εἰκ. 1.

[12] For the antiquities of Dekeleia see F. Willemsen, "Vom Grabbezirk des Nikodemos in Dekeleia," *MDAI(A)* 89 (1974), pp. 173-191. Of the objects which he presents in his plates, numbers 71-78 were not there, nor were they visible in the photograph of the museum.

CHAPTER TWO

DESCRIPTION

The three decrees which comprise the inscription are inscribed on both sides of a *stele* of fine-grained white marble. The *stele* is broken at the bottom. Its preserved height is 0.886 m. A molding, consisting of a fascia above an ovolo, crowns the *stele*. On the fascia, carved in low relief, are two olive sprays, which run in from either edge to meet at the center. Traces of green paint (perhaps modern?) survive on the molding. The molding measures 0.086 m. high, 0.405 m. wide and 0.075 m. thick. Immediately beneath the molding the *stele* measures 0.393 m. wide. The width of the stone flares slightly below to the bottom, where it measures 0.405 m. wide. The *stele* is uniformly 0.065 m. thick. All four of its vertical edges have been bevelled; its top has been roughly finished with a claw chisel; its two vertical sides have been smoothly finished.

The letters of the inscription's heading (line 1) measure between 0.014 m. and 0.017 m. in height. In contrast, the letters from the section describing the "priestly perquisites" (lines 2-12) vary from 0.008 m. to 0.01 m. in height. The text of this section is inscribed in the *stoichedon* arrangement, 25 letters per line. The *stoichedon* grid here measures 0.015 m. square.

The letters of the first decree, that of Hierokles (lines 13-68), are smaller, varying from a minimum height of 0.006 m. to a maximum of 0.008 m. The *stoichedon* grid is compressed here to allow 30 letters per line, so measuring vertically 0.013 m. and horizontally 0.012 m. The *stoichedon* arrangement is violated at lines 19, 20, 22, 30 and 56, for all of which see the Epigraphical Notes below.

The decree of Hierokles begins on the *recto* of the *stele* (lines 13-58) and ends on the *verso* (lines 59-68). The *stoichedon* grid continues without change from one face of the inscription to the other, until line 68 where the decree of Hierokles ends and the decree of Nikodemos begins. In this, the second decree (lines 68-113), the letters are identical in size and hand to those of the decree of Hierokles. The *stoichedon* grid, however, changes subtly, now measuring 0.012 m. square. The grid is not observed at all in the large erasure (lines 69-73), and is also violated in lines 72, 100, 104 and 106, for all of which see the Epigraphical Notes below.

The final decree, that of Menexenos (lines 114-126), is not carved according to the *stoichedon* arrangement. The letters here are slightly larger than those of the previous two decrees, measuring a fairly constant 0.01 m. The lines vary from 32 to 38 letters in length.

BIBLIOGRAPHY

I have collected here only those essays which pertain to the text, restorations, physical appearance or provenience of the stone. Independent editions of the text are listed first, in chronological order; other essays follow, enclosed in square brackets.

S. Koumanoudes, "Ψήφισμα Φρατερικόν," *ArchEph* (1883), cols. 69-76; U. Köhler, *apud IG* II, 2 (addenda), 841 b (1883); H. Lolling, " Ἀνασκαφαὶ καὶ εὑρήματα ἐν Δεκελεία," *AD* 4 (1888), pp. 159-163; J. Pantazides, " Ἐπιγραφὴ ἐκ Δεκελείας," *ArchEph* (1888), pp. 1-20; U. Köhler, *IG* II, 5, 841 b (1895); Th. Arvanitopoulou, Δεκελεία (Πολέμων, παράρτημα), Athens 1958.

[A. Milchhöfer, "Antikenbericht aus Attika," *Ath. Mit.* 12 (1887), p. 320 no. 428; F.B. Tarbell, "The Decrees of the Demotionidai, a Study of the Attic Phratry," *Papers of the American School in Athens* 5 (1886-1890), pp. 170-188; W.R. Paton, "Comment on Tarbell's 'Study of an Attic Phratry,' " *AJA* 6 (1890), pp. 314-318; F.B. Tarbell, "Mr. Tarbell's Reply to Mr. Paton's Comment," *AJA* 6 (1890), pp. 318-320; H. Sauppe, "Commentatio de phratriis altera," *Index scholarum in Academia Georgia Augusta*, 1890; W.R. Paton, "The Decelean Inscription and Attic Phratries," *CR* 5 (1891), pp. 221-223; Th. Arvanitopoulou, with Sophia and Eirene, Princesses of Greece, Ὄστρακα ἐκ Δεκελείας, Athens 1959.]

TEXT:[1]

FACE A:

Διὸς Φρατρίο
ἱερεὺς « «Θεόδωρος» Εὐφα«ντίδ»ο ^{ν ν}» ἀν
ἔγραψε καὶ ἔστησε τὴν στήλην. ^ν
ἱερεώσυνα τῶι ἱερεῖ διδόναι τ
5   άδε· ἀπὸ τὸ μείο κωλῆν, πλευρόν, ὀ
      ς, ἀργυρίο |||. ^ν ἀπὸ τὸ κορείο κωλῆ
      ν, πλευρόν, ὀς, ἐλατῆρα χοινικια
      ῖον, οἴνο ἡμίχον, ἀργυρίο | . ^{ν ν ν ν}
      τάδε ἔδοξεν τοῖς φράτερσι ἐπὶ
10   Φορμίωνος ἄρχοντος Ἀθηναίοι
      ς, φρατριαρχὸντος δὲ Παντακλέ
      ος ἐξ Οἴο. ^{vacant 18}
      Ἱεροκλῆς εἶπε· ὁπόσοι μήπω διεδικάσ
      θησαν κατὰ τὸν νόμον τὸν Δημοτιωνιδ
15   ῶν, διαδικάσαι περὶ αὐτῶν τὸς φράτερ
      ας αὐτίκα μάλα, ὑποσχομένος πρὸς τὸ Δ
      ιὸς τὸ Φρατρίο, φέροντας τὴν ψῆφον ἀπ
      ὸ τὸ βωμὸ. ὃς δ' ἂν δόξηι μὴ ὢν φράτηρ ἐσα
      χθῆναι, ἐξαλειψάτω τὸ ὄνομα αὐτὸ ὁ ἱερ
20   εὺς καὶ ὁ φρατρίαρχος ἐκ τὸ γραμματεί
      ο τὸ ἐν Δημοτιωνιδῶν καὶ τὸ ἀντιγράφ
      ο. ὁ δὲ ἐσαγαγὼν τὸν ἀποδικασθέντα ὀφε
      ιλέτω ἑκατὸν δραχμὰς ἱερὰς τῶι Διὶ τ
      ῶι Φρατρίωι· ἐσπράττεν δὲ τὸ ἀργύριο
25   ν τοῦτο τὸν ἱερέα καὶ τὸν φρατρίαρχο
      ν, ἢ αὐτὸς ὀφείλεν. τὴν δὲ διαδικασίαν
      τὸ λοιπὸν ἔναι τῶι ὑστέρωι ἔτει ἢ ὧι ἂ
      ν τὸ κόρεον θύσηι, τῆι Κορεώτιδι Ἀπατ
      ορίων· φέρεν δὲ τὴν ψῆφον ἀπὸ τὸ βωμὸ. ἐ
30   ἀν δέ τις βόληται ἐφεῖναι ἐς Δημοτιων
      ίδας ὧν ἂν ἀποψηφίσωνται, ἐξεῖναι αὐ

---

[1] Most of the editorial conventions which I use will be familiar to the reader. Some, perhaps, will not have encountered the use of double angled brackets, «...», which surround letters carved *in rasura*. For these signs and all others, consult H. Krummrey and S. Panciera, "Criteri di edizione e segni diacritici," *Tituli* 2 (1980), pp. 205-215.

τῶι· ἑλέσθαι δὲ ἐπ' αὐτοῖς συνηγόρος τ
ὸν Δεκελειῶν οἶκον πέντε ἄνδρας ὑπὲ
ρ τριάκοντα ἔτη γεγονότας, τούτος δὲ
35 ἐξορκωσάτω ὁ φρατρίαρχος καὶ ὁ ἱερε
ὺς συνηγορήσεν τὰ δικαιότατα καὶ ὀκ
ἐάσεν ὀδένα μὴ ὄντα φράτερα φρατρίζ
εν. ὅτο δ'ἂν τῶν ἐφέντων ἀποψηφίσωντα
ι Δημοτιωνίδαι, ὀφειλέτω χιλίας δρα
40 χμὰς ἱερὰς τῶι Διὶ τῶι Φρατρίωι, ἐσπρ
αττέτω δὲ τὸ ἀργύριον τοῦτο ὁ ἱερεὺς
τõ Δεκελειῶν οἴκο, ἢ αὐτὸς ὀφειλέτω. ἐ
ξεῖναι δὲ καὶ ἄλλωι τῶι βολομένωι τῶ
ν φρατέρων ἐσπράττεν τῶι κοινῶι. ταῦ
45 [τ]α δ' ἔναι ἀπὸ Φορμίωνος ἄρχοντος. ἐπι
ψηφίζεν δὲ τὸν φρατρίαρχον περὶ ὧν ἂ
ν «διαδικά»ζεν δέηι κατὰ τὸν ἐνιαυτὸν
ἕκαστον. ἐὰν δὲ μὴ ἐπιψηφίσηι, ὀφελέτ
ω πεντακοσία[s] δραχμὰς ἱερὰς τῶι Διὶ
50 [τ]ῶι Φρατρίω[ι. ἐ]σπράττεν δὲ τὸν ἱερέα
[κ]αὶ ἄλλο[ν τὸν βο]λόμενον τὸ ἀργύριον
τοῦτ[ο τῶι κοινῶι.] τὸ δὲ λοιπὸν ἄγεν τὰ
[μεῖα καὶ τὰ κόρει]α ἐς Δεκέλειαν ἐπὶ τ
[ὸν βωμόν. ἐὰν δὲ μὴ θ]ύσηι ἐπὶ τõ βωμõ, ὀφ
55 [ειλέτω πεντήκοντ]α δραχμὰς ἱερὰς τῶ
[ι Διὶ τῶι Φρατρίωι, ἐ]σπραττέτω δὲ ὁ ἱερ
[εὺς τὸ ἀργύριον τοῦτο] ἢ αὐτὸς ὀφειλέ
[τω ---------------²⁸---------------]

FACE B:

ἐὰν δέ τι τούτων διακωλύηι, ὅποι ἂν ὁ ἱ
60 ερεὺς προγράφηι, ἐνθαῦτα ἄγεν τὰ μεῖ
α καὶ τὰ κόρεια. προγράφεν δὲ προπέμπ
τα τῆς Δορπίας ἐν πινακίωι λελευκωμ
ένωι μὴ 'λατον ἢ σπιθαμιαίωι ὅπο ἂν Δ
εκελειῆς προσφοιτῶσιν ἐν ἄστει. τὸ δ
65 ὲ ψήφισμα τόδε καὶ τὰ ἱερεώσυνα ἀναγ

ράψαι τὸν ἱερέα ἐν στήληι λιθίνηι πρ
όσθεν τõ βωμõ Δεκελειᾶσιν τέλεσι το
ῖς ἑαυτõ. Νικόδημος εἶπε· τὰ μὲν ἄλλα κατ
«ὰ τὰ πρότερα ψηφίσματα, ἃ κēται περὶ τ»
70 «ēς εἰσαγωγῆς τῶν παίδων καὶ τῆς διαδ»
«ικασίας. τὸς δὲ μάρτυρας τρēς, ὃς εἴρη»
«ται ἐπὶ τῆι ἀνακρίσει παρέχεσθαι ἐκ τ»
«ῶν ἑαυτõ θιασωτῶν μαρτυρõντας τὰ ὑπερωτώμε(να)»
καὶ ἐπομνύντας τὸν Δία τὸν Φράτριον.
75 μαρτυρēν δὲ τὸς μάρτυρας καὶ ἐπομνύ
ναι ἐχομένος τõ βωμõ. ἐὰν δὲ μὴ ὦσι ἐν τ
ῶ<ι> θιάσωι τότωι τοσõτοι τὸν ἀριθμόν, ἐ
κ τῶν ἄλλων φρατέρων παρεχέσθω. ὅταν
δὲ ἦι ἡ διαδικασία, ὁ φρατρίαρχος μὴ π
80 ρότερον διδότω τὴν ψῆφον περὶ τῶν παί
δων τοῖς ἅπασι φράτερσι, πρὶν ἂν οἱ αὐ
τõ τõ εἰσαγομένο θιασῶται κρύβδην ἀ
πὸ τõ βωμõ φέροντες τὴν ψῆφον διαψηφ
ίσωνται. καὶ τὰς ψήφος τὰς τότων ἐναν
85 τίον τῶν ἀπάντων φρατέρων τῶν παρόν
των ἐν τῆι ἀγορᾶι ὁ φρατρίαρχος διαρ
ιθμησάτω καὶ ἀναγορευέτω ὁπότερ' ἂν
ψηφίσωνται. ἐὰν δὲ ψηφισαμένων τῶν θ
ιασωτῶν ἐναι αὐτοῖς φράτερα οἱ ἄλλο
90 ι φράτερες ἀποψηφίσωνται, ὀφειλόντ
ων ἑκατὸν δραχμὰς ἱερὰς τῶι Διὶ τῶι Φ
ρατρίωι οἱ θιασῶται, πλὴν ὅσοι ἂν τῶν
θιασωτῶν κατήγοροι ἢ ἐναντιόμενοι
φαίνωνται ἐν τῆι διαδικασίαι. ἐὰν δὲ
95 ἀποψηφίσωνται οἱ θιασῶται, ὁ δὲ εἰσά
γων ἐφῆι εἰς τὸς ἅπαντας, τοῖς δὲ ἅπασ
ι δόξει ἐναι φράτηρ, ἐνγραφέσθω εἰς τ
ὰ κοινὰ γραμματεῖα. ἐὰν δὲ ἀποψηφίσω
νται οἱ ἅπαντες, ὀφειλέτω ἑκατὸν δρα
100 χμὰς ἱερὰς τῶι Διὶ τῶι Φρατρίωι. ἐὰν δὲ
ἀποψηφισαμένων τῶν θιασωτῶν μὴ ἐφῆ
ι εἰς τὸς ἅπαντας, κυρία ἔστω ἡ ἀποψήφ
ισις ἡ τῶν θιασωτῶν. οἱ δὲ θιασῶται με
τὰ τῶν ἄλλων φρατέρων μὴ φερόντων τὴν

105 ψῆφον περὶ τῶν παίδων τῶν ἐκ τõ θιάσο
τõ ἑαυτῶν. τὸ δὲ ψήφισμα τόδε προσαναγ
ραψάτω ὁ ἱερεὺς εἰς τὴν στήλην τὴν λι
θίνην. ὅρκος μαρτύρων ἐπὶ τῆι εἰσαγω
γεῖ τῶν παίδων· μαρτυρῶ ὃν εἰσάγει ἑα
110 υτῶι υὸν ἔναι τõτον γνήσιον ἐγ γαμετ
ῆς· ἀληθῆ ταῦτα νὴ τὸν Δία τὸν Φράτριο
ν· εὐορκõ<ν>τι μέν μοι πολλὰ καὶ ἀγαθὰ ἐν
«αι, εἰ δ'» ἐπιορκοίην, τἀναντία. ^vacant 7
Μενέξενος εἶπεν· δεδόχθαι τοῖς φράτερσι περὶ
115 τῆς εἰσαγωγῆς τῶμ παίδων τὰ μὲν ἄλλα κα
τὰ τὰ πρότερα ψηφίσματα, ὅπως δ' ἂν εἰδῶσι οἱ
φράτερες τοὺς μέλλοντας εἰσάγεσθαι, ἀπο
γράφεσθαι τῶι πρώτωι ἔτει ἢ ὧι ἂν τὸ κούρεο
ν ἄγει τὸ ὄνομα πατρόθεγ καὶ τõ δήμου καὶ τῆ
120 ς μητρὸς πατρόθεν καὶ τοῦ [δ]ήμου πρὸς τὸν
φρατρίαρχον, τὸν δὲ φρατρία[ρχον ἀπογραψ]
αμένων ἀναγράψαντα ἐκ[τιθέναι ὅπου ἂν Δεκ]
ελέες προσφοιτῶσι, ἐκτιθ[έναι δὲ καὶ τὸν ἱερέα]
ἀναγράψαντα ἐν σανιδ[ίωι λευκῶι ἐν τῶι ἱερ]
125 ῶι τῆς Λητοῦς. τὸ δὲ φρ[ατερικὸν ψήφισμα ἀναγρ]
[άψαι εἰς τὴν σ]τήλην [τὴν λιθίνην τὸν ἱερέα ---]

APP. CRIT.

Line 52: Koumanoudes 1883.
Line 53: Köhler 1883.
Line 54: Köhler 1883.
Line 55: Koumanoudes 1883.
Line 56: Koumanoudes 1883. τῶ[ι Διὶ τῶι ʿΕρκείωι, ἐ]σπραττέτω Paton 1890.
Line 57: Köhler 1883. ἱερ[εὺς τõ Δεκελειῶν οἴκο] Koumanoudes 1883. ἱερ[εὺς τῶν Δημοτιωνιδῶν] Paton 1890.
Line 58: ὀφειλέ[τω, εἰ μὴ λοιμός τις ἔσται ἢ πόλεμος] Sauppe 1890.
Line 121: Pantazides 1888.
Line 122: Pantazides 1888.
Line 123: Lolling 1888. ἐκτιθ[έναι δὲ καὶ τὰ ὀνόματα] Pantazides 1888.

Line 124:   Lolling 1888.   σανιδί[ωι λελευκωμένωι] ΟΙΤΗΣΛΗΤΟΥΣ
Pantazides 1888.
Lines 125-126:   Hedrick.   ψ[ήφισμα τόδε ἀναγράψαι] Köhler 1895,
Lolling 1888.   [εἰς τὴν] στήλην [τὴν λιθίνην] Lolling 1888.

EPIGRAPHICAL NOTES

Lines 1-113:   Though the *stoichedon* pattern changes three times in this
section (lines 2-12, 13-68 and 68-113), all of these lines were carved by the
same hand.

Line 2:   It will be apparent from the photograph that there have been
two *consecutive* erasures within the seventeen *stoichoi* after ΙΕΡΕΥΣ. At some
time after the initial inscription of the stone, *stoichoi* 7-23 were erased. Then,
later yet, a part of this erasure was again erased: *stoichoi* 7-12 and 17-20 have
been erased to a perceptibly greater depth than the rest of the erasure. As
there have been two erasures, it is clear that three names have been carved
in this space.

The first name to be inscribed must have conformed to the stoichedon
arrangement of the rest of the inscription, and occupied the entire available
space. So it is possible to reconstruct the name originally inscribed: [--^{17}--].

The length of the second name to occupy the erasure may be
reconstructed with some confidence. Since *stoichoi* 17-20 were later erased,
it may be taken as certain that the second name must have extended *at least*
to *stoichos* 20. The name may have conceivably extended to *stoichos* 21, if we
presume that the *omikron* in that place was originally part of the second name,
and was reused by the stonemason in carving the third name. The second
name *cannot* have extended into *stoichoi* 22 and 23, since these have only been
erased once and are blanks.

The first four letters of the patronymic of the second name, ΕΥΦΑ, have
been reused to make the patronymic of the third name. It is certain that these
letters are reused, because they are inscribed in the first erasure, and are
flanked on either side by the second erasure.

The four surviving letters of the second name are tidily cut and are
properly aligned with the *stoichedon* grid of this section of the inscription.
The second name to stand in the erasure, then, conformed to the pre-existing
stoichedon grid of the inscription.

The second name to stand within this erasure may thus be reconstructed
with accuracy: either [......] ΕΥΦΑ[....]Ο $^{v\,v}$ or [......] ΕΥΦΑ[....] $^{v\,v\,v}$. The

sections of the name which I here enclose in square brackets are those *stoichoi* which have been twice erased.

The third name to stand in this erasure, Θεόδωρος Εὐφαντίδο, had the first four letters of its patronymic in common with the patronymic of the second name. For this reason the stonemason evidently decided to reuse the appropriate letters of the patronymic. To accomodate the arrangement, the eight letters of the name Θεόδωρος had to be squeezed into the six *stoichoi* previously occupied by the second name. This decision, of course, abused the *stoichedon* arrangement of the text. It was, furthermore, an unnecessarily sloppy solution: had the stonecutter erased the second name entirely and then inscribed the third, Θεόδωρος Εὐφαντίδο, he would have precisely filled the 17 *stoichoi* available within the erasure.

The letters which have been cut in the second erasure, ΘΕΟΔΩΡΟΣ and ΝΤΙΔ, were not cut by the same mason who carved the perquisites and first two decrees: in general they are more carelessly made. This sloppiness can best be seen in the shapes of the Δ and E: not even the *hastae* of these letters are uniformly straight. The difference of hand can also be illustrated by the design of the S and O: the top and bottom *hastae* of the Σ flare far more than is usual in the first two decrees; the arc of the O is more elliptical than elsewhere.

Line 3: At the end of the line, one blank space has been left.

Line 6: The three vertical *hastae* denoting obols have been crowded into one *stoichos*, and a blank space has been left immediately after them.

Line 8: Four blank spaces have been left at the end of the line.

Line 12: The 18 spaces at the end of this line have been left blank.

Line 19: This line contains 31 letters, one more than the *stoichedon* pattern will allow. Instead of doubling two letters into one space, as he does elsewhere, the stonecutter has recast the distribution of letters in the entire line: for the first three and last five spaces of the line, the letters fall squarely into the vertical rows of the *stoichedon* grid; the rest of the letters have been evenly distributed throughout the line with no regard for the *stoichedon* pattern. At the eighth *stoichos*, the Ξ falls into line, apparently by chance; elsewhere the letters are consistently and deliberately set out of the vertical alignment.

Line 20: An extra letter has been absorbed into this line by compressing the last three letters, ΤΕΙ, into two spaces.

Line 22: The extra letter in this line has been accommodated by carving eight letters in the center of the line, ΓΩΝΤΟΝΑΠ, into six spaces.

Line 30: An extra letter has been absorbed into this line by combining A and I in the third *stoichos*.

Line 47: Beginning with the second *stoichos*, ΔΙΑΔΙΚΑ has been carved *in rasura*.

Line 52: Only the top bar of the Ṭ, the top arc of the Ọ and the right half of the top of the second Ṭ are preserved.

Line 53: The right bar of the Ạ is visible.

Line 56: The line is restored with 31 letters, one more than the *stoichedon* pattern will allow. The restoration is impeccable (see below, Chapter 3, commentary *ad loc.*), and I would account for the extra letter by either assuming the omission of an I in one of the dative endings (cf. line 77), or better, the combination into one *stoichos* of an I with a neighboring letter (cf. lines 20, 30 and 68). So, for example, the two iotas of Διί might be cut in one space. In this line, only the top *hasta* of the Σ̣ is preserved.

Line 57: Only the tops of the two vertical *hastae* of the Ḥ are preserved.

Line 68: Two extra letters have been placed in the line by the combination of the EI of εἶπε into one space, and by cutting the last three letters, KAT, into two spaces.

Lines 69-73: These five lines have been cut *in rasura*. The vertical grid of lines 69-74 has been compressed to 0.010 m., so fitting six lines into a space that would originally have been occupied by five lines with a vertical grid of 0.012 m. In line 72 an additional letter, T, has been added at the end of the line, outside of the *stoichedon* pattern. Line 73 contains 37 letters. Moreover, the stonecutter, because of lack of space, has left the last word of the line incomplete. With the two missing letters, there are nine excessive letters in the line. The first three letters of the line stand directly in the vertical *stoichedon* rows, as do the letters in the 27th through the 30th spaces. The last letter of the line, E, falls under the T of the line above, outside of the *stoichedon* grid. The rest of the letters of the line have been crammed together with more regard for economy of space than for the *stoichedon* pattern.

The lines have been placed in the erasure more closely than in the rest of the decree of Nikodemos, so as to provide for an extra line. The thirty letters gained by the manoeuvre were not sufficient to contain the additional material which the stonecutter wished to inscribe. In the first four lines of the erasure he maintained the *stoichedon* pattern, but when he arrived at the fifth he found himself with an extra 10 letters. To solve the problem he carved one of the letters at the end of the preceding line, outside of the *stoichedon* grid. He was able to eliminate six more by compressing the distribution of letters in the line. The eighth letter he carved at the end of the line, beneath its mate from the preceding line, outside of the *stoichedon* pattern. Despite these measures, he still found himself with two extra letters, which he omitted.

Line 77: The stone cutter has neglected to cut an I at the end of the dative article.

Line 100: Three letters, PAΣ, have been carved in the seventh and eighth *stoichoi*.

Line 104: The final letter of the line, N, has been carved outside of the *stoichedon* grid.

Line 106: Three letters, POΣ, have been compressed to fit into the 25th and 26th spaces of this line.

Line 113: The decree of Nikodemos ends in the middle of the line, and the last seven spaces have been left blank. The first five letters of the line are cut *in rasura*.

Lines 114-126: The decree of Menexenos has been cut by a different hand.

Line 120: Of the Ḥ, only the tops of the two *hastae* and a part of the horizontal are visible.

Line 124: Only the two slanting bars of the Δ̣ are visible.

Line 125: Only the top part of the Λ̣ is preserved.

Line 126: Only the horizontal bar of the Ṭ is visible. Of the Ḥ, only the tops of the vertical *hastae* may be seen. The crux of the Λ̣ may yet be seen. Only the top left stroke of the Ṇ is visible.

TRANSLATION:

FACE A:

(*Stele*) of Zeus Phratrios.

The priest, Theodoros son of Euphantides, had the *stele* inscribed and erected. The following shall be given to the priest as his perquisites: from the *meion* a haunch, a flank, an ear and three silver *obols*; from the *koureion* a haunch, a flank, an ear, a cake weighing one *choinix*, half a *chous* of wine and one *drachma*.

The *phrateres* decreed the following in the year in which Phormion was archon in Athens and the phratriarch was Pantakles from Oion:

Hierokles proposed: So many as have not yet undergone the scrutiny in accordance with the law of the Demotionidai, the *phrateres* shall scrutinize them immediately. The *phrateres* shall swear by Zeus Phratrios, and they shall take their ballots from the altar. If it is decided that someone has been introduced to the phratry though not entitled, the priest and the phratriarch shall erase his name from the archive in the sanctuary of the Demotionidai and from the copy. Further, let the person who originally sponsored the one who has not undergone the scrutiny owe one hundred *drachmai*, which shall be consecrated to Zeus Phratrios. This money the priest and phratriarch shall exact, or they shall themselves owe it. The scrutiny shall in the future be conducted in the year after the sacrifice of the *koureion*, at the festival of the Apatouria, on the day called *Koureotis*. The ballot shall be taken from the altar. Should one of those whom they have expelled wish to appeal to the Demotionidai, he shall be allowed. The House of the Dekeleians shall choose as advocates in these cases five men over thirty years old. Let the phratriarch and the priest administer an oath to these men "to act as advocates justly, and not to permit anyone who is not entitled to continue to exercize the privileges of a *phrater*." Whomever of the appellants the Demotionidai reject, let him owe a thousand *drachmai* which shall be consecrated to Zeus Phratrios, and let the priest of the House of the Dekeleians exact the money, or let him owe it himself. Any of the *phrateres* who wishes shall be permitted to exact the money for the group. The preceding shall be in effect from the archonship of Phormion. The phratriarch shall put it to the vote annually whether they need to scrutinize anyone. Should he not put it to the vote, let him owe five hundred *drachmai*, which shall be consecrated to Zeus Phratrios. The priest and anyone else who wishes shall exact the money for the group. In the future, the *meia* and the *koureia* shall be celebrated at Dekeleia on the altar. If anyone should not sacrifice on the altar, let him owe fifty *drachmai* which shall be consecrated to Zeus Phratrios. Let the priest exact the money or owe it himself.

[---]

FACE B:

...if one of these things should prove a hindrance, then the *meia* and the *koureia* shall be celebrated at the place which the priest shall post. The priest shall post his notice five days before the day *Dorpia*, on a white-washed board, no smaller than a span, at the place in the city where the Dekeleians meet.

The text of this decree and of the priestly perquisites the priest shall have inscribed on a marble *stele* in front of the altar at Dekeleia at his own expense.

Nikodemos proposed: Let everything else be in accordance with the previous decrees which have been passed concerning the introduction of children and the scrutiny, but as for the three witnesses whom the regulations prescribe for the preliminary examination, he shall furnish them from among his own *thiasotai*, and they shall give testimony to the questions posed, and shall swear by Zeus Phratrios. The witnesses shall testify and swear holding to the altar. If there should not be so many members in his *thiasos*, let him furnish them from the other *phrateres*. Whenever there is a scrutiny, let the phratriarch not call for a vote concerning the children in the full assembly of the *phrateres* before the *thiasotai* of the child being introduced have secretly voted, taking their ballots from the altar. Let the phratriarch, in the presence of all the *phrateres* who are present at the meeting place, count their ballots and let him announce which way they have voted. If the *thiasotai* vote that he is their *phrater* and the rest of the *phrateres* reject him, let the *thiasotai* owe one hundred *drachmai*, which shall be consecrated to Zeus Phratrios, except for those of the *thiasotai* who appear to have spoken against the admission, or to have opposed it at the scrutiny. But if the *thiasotai* reject him and the sponsor appeals to the full assembly, and the full assembly decrees that he is entitled to admission, then let him be enrolled on the common registers. But if all reject him, let him pay one hundred *drachmai*, which shall be consecrated to Zeus Phratrios. If the *thiasotai* reject him and he does not appeal to the full assembly, then let the rejection pronounced by the *thiasotai* be final. Let the *thiasotai* not vote in the full assembly when the vote concerns children from their own *thiasos*. Let the priest have this decree also inscribed on the marble *stele*.

The oath of the witnesses at the introduction of the children: "I testify that the child whom he sponsors is his legitimate son, born of his lawful wife. These things are true, by Zeus Phratrios. If I swear truly, may it be well with me; if falsely, the opposite."

Menexenos proposed: That the *phrateres* decree that, concerning the introduction of children, let everything else be in accordance with the previous decrees; but so that the *phrateres* may know who is about to be introduced, let a deposition be made to the phratriarch in the first year, or that in which he celebrates the *koureion*, a deposition of his name, patronymic, demotic, and the name and demotic of his mother's father. The phratriarch, after the depositions have been made, shall have the names inscribed and shall have them displayed at the place where the Dekeleians meet. The priest shall also have the list displayed, having it written up on a white-washed board in the sanctuary of Leto. Let the priest have the phratry decree inscribed on the marble *stele*....

[--]

CHAPTER THREE

GENERAL COMMENTARY

ORGANIZATION OF THE INSCRIPTION

The "Inscription of the Demotionidai" may be divided into seven sections: the heading (line 1); the record of the erection of the *stele* (lines 2-3); the list of priestly perquisites (lines 4-8); the preamble, which is comprised of the formulaic decree and date (lines 9-12); the decree of Hierokles (lines 13-68); the decree of Nikodemos (lines 68-113); and the decree of Menexenos (lines 114-126).

The various parts of the text were inscribed on three distinguishable occasions. On the first occasion, most of the face A and part of face B were inscribed: the "priestly perquisites" and the decree of Hierokles are specifically mentioned in the publication order at lines 64-66; the heading, record of erection and preamble must be tacitly included in this order. The decree of Nikodemos was published a short while later; the order to have it published is given at line 106. The decree of Menexenos was inscribed long afterward, perhaps in the 360's. The order to have it published is restored in lines 125-126.

These units are paralleled and confirmed by the physical layout of the text on the stone. The first unit, the heading of the decree, stands physically and syntactically independent of what follows. It is inscribed apart from the body of the text, in larger letters on the crowning molding.

The second section (lines 2-3) begins with the second line. It records that the priest had the *stele* inscribed and erected. One blank *stoichos*, the last of line 3, is left at the end of this unit.

The third section (lines 4-8) begins with the fourth line. It describes the dues derived by the priest from the two sacrifices of the *meion* and *koureion*. One blank *stoichos* in line 6 has been used to divide the respective lists of perquisites due from each sacrifice. This section stops four *stoichoi* from the end of line 8; these spaces have been left blank.

The fourth section (lines 9-12), which records the formulaic decree of the *phrateres* and the date of the inscription, begins with a new line. It ends in the seventh *stoichos* of line 12. The stonemason has left the rest of that line, 18 *stoichoi*, uninscribed.

The fifth section, the decree of Hierokles (lines 9-68), begins with a new line. It continues past the end of face A onto face B. No blank space has been left at the end of this section.

The sixth section of the inscription, the decree of Nikodemos (lines 68-113), takes up immediately where the decree of Hierokles leaves off. It ends in line 126. The stonemason has left the end of that line, 7 *stoichoi*, uninscribed.

The final section of the document, the decree of Menexenos (lines 114-126), begins with a new line. The stone unfortunately breaks off before the end of the section.

SECTION 1: THE HEADING

Line 1: With the genitive of the divinity's name should be understood the phrase ἡ στήλη ἱερά. The *stele* is a holy offering. It is erected "in front of the altar of Zeus Phratrios" (line 66), so it is devoted to and in the protection of that divinity.[1]

Zeus Phratrios is ubiquitous in the regulations of this phratry. Oaths are sworn in his name, fines levied are consecrated to him and it is on his altar that the initiation sacrifices are made (lines 16, 24, 40, 50, 56, 74, 91, 100 and 111). So far as the evidence goes, he is the chief and solitary divinity of this phratry.

It is curious that the inscription nowhere mentions either of the other gods most commonly associated with the Attic phratry: Athena Phratria and Apollo Patroios. Athena Phratria was often worshipped in conjunction with Zeus Phratrios. The ancestral Apollo, Apollo Patroios, is also absent from these decrees. The only divinity mentioned in this inscription besides Zeus is a minor, idiosyncratic goddess of this phratry, Leto (line 125).[2] This exclusion

---

[1] See *SIG*³ 1021, line 1; 1100, line 1; *Olympia, Inschriften*, no. 2, line 9; A. Wilhelm, "Zu griechischen Inschriften," *AEMOe* 20 (1897), pp. 91-92. M.A. Flower, "*IG* II² 2344 and the Size of Phratries in Classical Athens," *CQ* 35 (1985), pp. 232-235; C.W. Hedrick, Jr., "The Phratry from Paiania," *CQ* 59 (1989), pp. 126-135.

[2] For the gods of the Attic phratries see generally Pollux 1, 24 and 3, 51. On Zeus and Athena Phratrios see U. Höfer, *RL* 3, 2 (1902-1909), Φράτριοι, cols. 2454-2457, and K. Latte, *RE* 20, 1 (1941), φράτριοι θεοί, cols. 756-758. For Apollo Patroos, see now C.W. Hedrick, Jr., "The Temple and Cult of Apollo Patroos in Athens," *AJA* 92 (1988), pp. 185-210; X. De Schutter, "Le culte d'Apollon Patrôos à Athènes," *AC* 56 (1987), pp. 103-129. For some examples of the worship of minor, idiosyncratic gods by Attic phratries, see, *e.g.*, C.W. Hedrick, Jr., "Old and New on the Attic Phratry of the Therrikleidai," *Hesperia* 52 (1983), pp. 299-302; *idem*, "The Thymaitian Phratry," *Hesperia* 57 (1988), pp. 81-85.

of other common phratry divinities is not unparalleled. At least two other phratries seem to have worshipped Zeus Phratrios alone.[3]

SECTION 2: ERECTION OF THE STELE

Lines 2-3: In lines 64-68 Hierokles requires that "the text of this decree and of the priestly perquisites the priest shall have inscribed on a marble *stele* at his own expense." From this provision it is clear that the *stele* was erected and everything through the end of the decree of Hierokles inscribed at the same time: that is, 396/5 (for the date, see the commentary to line 10 below).

The phratry priest did indeed have the decree and the priestly perquisites inscribed, but not in the order which Hierokles specified. The list of perquisites was cut ahead of the decree. In addition this line, which boldly advertises that the priest had the *stele* erected and inscribed, has been inserted near the head of the inscription. The priest's name and title now appear in the second line, directly below the name of the god. The prominence given to the priest and his functions is surely due to the preferences of the agent charged with the erection of the *stele*, that is, the priest himself.[4]

Virtually all of our knowledge of priests in the Attic phratry derives from this inscription. The literary sources say nothing about the role of the phratry priest, and little supplementary information is provided by other inscriptions: one fragmentary inscription mentions a phratry's priest and perhaps his perquisites;[5] another inscription preserves an isolated reference to perquisites.[6]

The priesthood was evidently a position of some power within this phratry. As we see here, the priest received some "perquisites" from phratry sacrifices. He was also responsible for determining where phratry celebrations might take place (line 60). He was charged with the erection of inscriptions which either were concerned with religious matters or were to stand in a

---

[3] One other phratry inscription and one other phratry altar are attested as devoted solely to Zeus Phratrios: respectively *IG* II^2 1239 and [Dem.] 43, 11-15, 81-83. See further the discussion of phratry altars below, commentary to lines 17-18.

[4] See *SIG*^{3} 921, note 34.

[5] *IG* II^2 1240; see A. Wilhelm, "'Αττικὰ Ψηφίσματα," *ArchEph* (1905), p. 227 note 7.

[6] M. Walbank, "Greek Inscriptions from the Athenian Agora, Fifth to Third Centuries B.C.," *Hesperia* 51 (1982), pp. 48-50 no. 7, line 9. For an revised text, see C.W. Hedrick, Jr., "Old and New on the Attic Phratry of the Therrikleidai," *Hesperia* 52 (1983), pp. 299-302.

sacred area (lines 66, 108, 126).[7] He might discipline those who transgressed the phratry's regulations (lines 55-57). With the phratriarch he administered oaths (lines 35-36), exacted fines (line 25) and supervised the phratry's records (lines 19-20). He might even collect fines from the phratriarch himself, if that official abused his position (line 50).

The name of the priest which is preserved here, Theodoros son of Euphantides, was the third name to be inscribed in this place (see above, Chapter 2, Epigraphic Notes to line 2). It is unlikely that the re-inscription of the name is due to a simple error of the stone cutter: there are certainly two *consecutive* erasures here; three *different* names have *consecutively* occupied the space; the last of these names was not inscribed by the same mason who cut the decrees of Hierokles and Nikodemos. This double erasure and triple inscription of the names may be most economically explained, I suggest, in terms of the serial, incremental publication of the decrees.

The document, as has been explained, was inscribed in three stages: first the priestly perquisites and the decree of Hierokles, then the decree of Nikodemos, and finally the decree of Menexenos. Each decree closes with an order that *the priest* have the decree inscribed. Presumably, as each decree was added to the stone, the priest responsible erased the name of his predecessor from line two, and had his own inscribed in its place.

At the end of the first decree, that of Hierokles, it is provided that "the priest shall have a *stele* erected and have inscribed on it the perquisites and this decree (lines 64-8). The first name to occupy this space, [........[17].......], was doubtless that of the priest who had these perquisites and the first decree inscribed in 396/5.

Later, at the end of the second decree, it is ordered that "the priest have this decree inscribed also on the marble stele (lines 106-8)." The priest who had the second decree inscribed was surely he whose name filled the first erasure: [......] Εὐφα[....]ο^{vv} or [......] Εὐφα[....]^{vvv}. A possible restoration of the patronymic of this second priest might be Εὐφά[νους]. It would be the first attestation of an Εὐφάνης for the deme of Dekeleia, but the name is common enough that this objection carries little weight.

Finally, the third decree was passed. Its end has been mutilated, but it may be assumed with confidence that the priest was required to "have this decree also inscribed on the marble stele." This third priest, Theodoros son

---

[7] The phratriarch was, in normal circumstances, charged with this duty: see below, commentary to lines 9-12. See in addition *IG* II^2 1240, lines 9-11; C.W. Hedrick, Jr., "Old and New on the Attic Phratry of the Therrikleidai," *Hesperia* 52 (1983), p. 300 note 5.

of Euphantides, followed precedent, having the name of his predecessor erased and his own inscribed in its place.

The common element Εὐφα- in the patronymics of the second and third priests points unmistakably to the conclusion that the two were members of the same family. Greek names are composed of component words. In a given family, names and components of names are often repeated.[8] If the two were related, as their names suggest, then it is a short leap to the conclusion that the priesthood was restricted to members of one family. It is scarcely surprising that the priesthood of a tribal organization such as the phratry should be gentilitial.

If I am correct in arguing that the priesthood of this phratry was restricted to a single family, then it is *a priori* probable that the office was held for life.[9] These decrees, however, were inscribed over a forty year period: the first in 396/5, the second soon after and the third in the 360's (see below, commentary to lines 9-12, 68 and 114). It might be objected that if the phratry's priesthood were held for life, then surely the same priest should have been in office for at least the span of time between the first two decrees, if not for that of all three. I would account for the speed and frequency of the hieratic succession by supposing that priests seldom survived for long after taking office. Seniority in the phratry was determined by rank within the family, that is, by age.[10] It is likely that the phratry's priesthood was held by the eldest member of the family which monopolized the office.

If my explanation of the unusual erasures of the name of the priest is correct, then the name "Theodoros son of Euphantides" was carved by the same hand as the third decree, that of Menexenos. This conclusion poses certain problems. Though the third name is clearly carved in a different hand than the first two decrees, there is insufficient evidence (only some 12 letters) to identify this hand with that of the decree of Menexenos (see Chapter 2,

---

[8] For the practice of repeating names and components of names in a family see E. Fränkel, *RE* 16, 2 (1935), Namenwesen, cols. 1624-1626. For an outstanding example of this phenomenon in the context of an Attic Phratry list, see *IG* II² 2344. Compare the commentary provided for this document in C.W. Hedrick, Jr., "The Phratry from Paiania," *CQ* 59 (1989), pp. 126-135.

[9] Priesthoods in ancient Greece might be held annually or for life. Gentilitial priesthoods were often inherited by the eldest male member of a family, and the principle implies tenure for life. See P. Stengel, *Die griechischen Kultusaltertümer* (*Handbuch der Altertumswissenschaft* 5, 3), Munich 1920, pp. 44-46.

[10] For the patriarchal character of the Greek family see, *e.g.*, W.K. Lacey, *The Family in Classical Greece*, Ithaca 1968, pp. 21-22. For the operation of this principle within the phratry see C.W. Hedrick, Jr., "The Phratry from Paiania," *CQ* 59 (1989), pp. 126-135.

Epigraphical Notes to line 2). Furthermore, though the so-called "false diphthong" is consistently observed in the decree of Menexenos, it is *not* observed in the genitive ending of Εὐφαντίδο.

I would account for these problems by suggesting that the stonemason who inscribed the name of the priest has tried to make his insertion conform to its surroundings. Though he ignored the *stoichedon* grid, he cut his letters to match roughly those of the earlier text. He has, I suggest, even modified the genitive ending of Εὐφαντίδο in order to match it to its surroundings. The stonemason might have been influenced in this decision by the genitive form of the deity's name, Διὸς Φρατρίο, which stands immediately above the name of the priest. In addition it should be noted that the period to which the third decree is assigned, the 360's, were years of transition over to the use of the "false diphthong" (see below, commentary to line 114). The stonemason surely was familiar and comfortable with both conventions for the representation of the diphthong.

If this argument is correct, then Theodoros was not the priest of the Demotionidai in 396/5 as has hitherto been supposed,[11] but rather in the 360's. Although his demotic is not directly attested, the prosopographical evidence and what we know of the geographic character of the phratry[12] combine to make it virtually certain that he was a demesman of Dekeleia.

The name of the father of Theodoros, Euphantides, is very rare. It is attested in only one other instance, as the name of a trierarch of the 370's: Εὐφαντίδης 'Αλ[---].[13] Davies, arguing from the rarity of the name, suggests the possibility of some relationship between the trierarch and the family of Theodoros; he concludes, however, that the nature of the relationship, given the difference in demes, must remain uncertain.[14]

Another explanation for the coincidence of these two names may now be suggested. Since Theodoros was priest in the 360's, and not in 396/5 as Davies supposed, his father and the trierarch were very close contemporaries: that is, both attestations of the name Euphantides date to the same generation. It may well be that the trierarch and the father of Theodoros were named for a popular personality of the day, and that no relationship between the two families existed.

---

[11] See *PA* 6861; Davies, *APF*, no. 6029.

[12] See *SIG*[3] 921, notes 3 and 25 and the commentary to lines 11-12 below.

[13] *IG* II[2] 1604, line 81.

[14] Davies, *APF*, no. 6029.

A certain Ἐκφαν[τί]δης Θεοδώρου Δεκελ[ε(ιεύς)] is attested as the lessee of a mine in an inscription of the second half of the fourth century B.C. The editor of the inscription took him to be the son of the priest of the Demotionidai, suggesting that a mistake had been made in one of the documents, a K being inscribed for an Ψ, or *vice versa*.[15] Such an emendation is unnecessary. The common components of the names Euphantides and Ekphantides, the recurrence of the name Theodoros, the Dekeleian demotic and the period of the mine lease combine to make it virtually certain that Ekphantides is the son of the phratry's priest. Again, the revised date for the priesthood of Theodoros fits much more tidily with the date of his son's mine lease.

Two other men from Dekeleia are known who may be relatives of the priest. One appears on a list of [---]ται from the second half of the fourth century.[16] On the list under the heading of Dekeleia occur the names (Σ)άννιος Στρατοκλέους, Θεόδωρος Στρατοκλέους and Πύθων Σαννίου. Another Dekeleian Θεόδωρος appears on a mortgage stone of 315/4.[17]

The formula used to describe the inscription and erection of the *stele* is common,[18] as might be expected, in providing for the publication of state documents in Athens (compare lines 64-8, 106-8, 125-6).

SECTION 3: THE PRIESTLY PERQUISITES

Line 4: Often certain parts of a sacrifice were allotted to the relevant priest as his due. The word denoting these priestly perquisites is ἱερεώσυνα.[19]

The names of many phratry sacrifices are attested. This document, however, lists the perquisites allotted the priest from only two of these, the *meion* and *koureion*. The omission of other sacrifices from this list does not imply that the priest collected no perquisites from them. The *meion* and

---

[15] So argues M. Crosby, "The Leases of the Laurion Mines," *Hesperia* 19 (1950), p. 267, no. 21, lines 11-12.

[16] *IG* II² 1927, lines 93-98. For the dubious nature of the list see D. Lewis, "Notes on Attic Inscriptions (II)," *ABS(A)* 50 (1955), p. 29; E. Ruschenbusch, "Die Diaitetenliste *IG* II/III² 1927," *ZPE* 49 (1982), pp. 267-281.

[17] *IG* II² 2725.

[18] For the formula, see L. Robert, "Communication: épigraphie et paléographie," *CRAI* (1955), pp. 216-217.

[19] On the form of the word ἱερεώσυνα and its variants ἱερώσυνα and ἱερειώσυνα see Threatte, *GAI* I, pp. 147-152, 154.

koureion alone are included because the decrees of this inscription are concerned with the admission of candidates to the phratry and these sacrifices were offered on such occasions.

The "priestly perquisites" of an Attic phratry are mentioned in one other inscription[20] and have been restored in another.[21] Unfortunately both documents are so fragmentary that they reveal virtually nothing of the circumstances of the sacrifice.

Lines 5-6: The sacrifice of the *meion* is attested only in the present inscription (see below, lines 53, 60-61 and the commentary to 118-119) and in the glosses of later scholiasts and lexicographers.[22] The evidence provided by this inscription is typically terse and sometimes controversial; the scholiastic glosses are often contradictory; nevertheless, the general character of the sacrifice is not disputed. The *meion* was offered on the third day of the Apatouria, *Koureotis* (see below, commentary to lines 28-29).[23] At the sacrifice, children born since the Apatouria of the previous year were presented to the phratry (see below, commentary to lines 118-119).[24]

The etymology of the name of the sacrifice, μεῖον, cannot at present be explained.[25] Before the discovery of this inscription, the word was attested only in the nominative and accusative singular. Accordingly, scholars concluded that it was a substantive neuter of the comparative adjective, μείων:

---

[20] M. Walbank, "Greek Inscriptions from the Athenian Agora, Fifth to Third Centuries B.C.," *Hesperia* 51 (1982), pp. 48-50 no. 7, line 9. Compare the comments of C.W. Hedrick, Jr., "Old and New on the Attic Phratry of the Therrikleidai," *Hesperia* 52 (1983), pp. 299-302.

[21] *IG* II^2 1240, line 3.

[22] On the *meion* see above all J. Labarbe, "L'age corréspondant au sacrifice du κούρειον et les données historiques du sixième discours d'Isée," *BAB* 39 (1953), pp. 361-362. The numerous citations of the scholiasts and lexicographers concerning this sacrifice are collected in C.W. Hedrick, Jr., *The Attic Phratry* (Thesis, University of Pennsylvania), Ann Arbor 1984, pp. 169-173. Probably the most important of these glosses is that preserved in the *Etymologicum Magnum s.v.* Ἀπατούρια.

[23] The relation between the day and sacrifice is explicitly stated only in the confused citation in the *Etymologicum Magnum, s.v.* κούρεον.

[24] It is nowhere explicitly stated that the *meion* was offered for children in their first year. Some of the later sources simply say that the *meion* was offered by fathers on behalf of their children: Schol. to Aristophanes, *Frogs*, 798; Harp. *s.v.* μεῖον; Photios *s.vv.* μεῖον, μειαγωγός; Pollux 3, 51-53. Others maintain that it is the equivalent of the *koureion*: Schol. to Aristophanes, *Frogs*, 798; *Etymologicum Magnum, s.v.* Κουρεῶτις; Suda *s.vv.* μειαγωγήσουσι, μειαγωγία.

[25] The suggestions of scholars have been reviewed by J. Labarbe, "L'age corréspondant au sacrifice du κούρειον et les données historiques du sixième discours d'Isée," *BAB* 39 (1953), p. 359 note 5.

"the lesser."[26] The sacrifice was lesser, it was explained, with reference to the *koureion*, which was sacrificed on the same day.

It is clear from the occurrences of the word in this inscription (lines 5, 53, 60-61) that μεῖον is a second declension noun. It therefore cannot be a nominal form of the comparative adjective μείων, and the older explanation of the word must be abandoned. No convincing replacement for this explanation has yet been proposed.[27]

The references to haunch, flank and ears among the priestly perquisites prove, if proof is necessary, that the ceremony of the *meion* included an animal sacrifice. It is not clear from the present context what animal is to be killed. According to the later scholiasts and lexicographers, however, the usual victim at the *meion* was a sheep.[28]

The flank (κωλήν) and haunch (πλευρόν) were the two parts of the victim most often given to the priest as his perquisites from a sacrifice.[29] It was less common, though by no means impossible, to assign an ear of the victim to the priest.[30]

---

[26] See for example A. Mommsen, *Heortologie, antiquarische Untersuchungen über die städtischen Feste der Athener*, Leipzig 1864, p. 308. Scholars were encouraged in this interpretation by the ancient glosses, which often espouse a similar etymology. According to the scholiasts and lexicographers, there was a law limiting the weight of the victim at the *meion*. Accordingly, when the sacrifice was weighed the hungry *phrateres*, hoping that it would be as close to the upper limit as possible, cried "μεῖον, μεῖον," "less, less." See Schol. to Aristophanes, *Frogs*, 798; *Etymologicum Magnum s.v.* Κουρεῶτις; Pollux 3, 51; Photios *s.vv.* μεῖον, μειαγωγός; Suda *s.vv.* μειαγωγήσουσι, μειαγωγία. Depending on how one interprets Aristophanes, this etymology may go as far back as the fifth century: see Aristophanes, *Frogs*, 797-798; Aristophanes, F. 286 Edm.

[27] This is not to say that no explanations have been proposed. For a review, see H. Frisk, *Griechisches etymologisches Wörterbuch*, 2v., Heidelberg 1960-1970, *s.v.* μεῖον.

[28] According to the Schol. to Aristophanes, *Frogs*, 798 an ὅϊς was sacrificed. Suda *s.vv.* μειαγωγήσουσι and μειαγωγία uses the more general πρόβατον. See G. Dindorff, ed., *Iulii Pollucis onomasticon*, Leipzig 1824, commentary to 3, 53.

[29] See J. Edmonds, *The Fragments of Attic Comedy*, Leiden 1957-1961, I, p. 480 F. 7 (=Athenaios 8, 368), a fragment of Ameipsias' victorious comedy of 423, the *Konnos*: δίδοται μάλισθ' ἱερεώσυνα κωλῆν, τὸ πλευρόν, ἡμίκραιφ' ἀριστερά. Compare further the remarks of Prott-Ziehen, *LGS* II, no. 17 p. 80; Sokolowski, *LSCG*, no. 19.

[30] A. Körte, "Mitgliederverzeichnis einer attischen Phratrie," *Hermes* 37 (1902), p. 587 note 2, suggested that the occurrence of the ear in the list of the priestly perquisites showed that the animal sacrificed here was a pig, claiming from experience that only a pig's ears were edible. It is known, however, that the ancient Greeks did occasionally assign the ears of animals other than pigs to the priest as his due: see Prott-Ziehen, *LGS* II, no. 17, p. 70 note 2; Sokolowski, *LSCG* no. 19.

Lines 6-8: The *koureion* was one of the most important phratry ceremonies.[31] Like the *meion* it took place on the third day of the Apatouria, a day to which it lent its name: *Koureotis*. This sacrifice was offered by fathers for their sons when the boys formally passed from childhood to adulthood and were introduced to the phratry.[32]

The decrees of the Demotionidai are the chief contemporary source of information about the ceremony of the *koureion* (see lines 6, 53, 62 and 118).[33] The ceremony is mentioned by name in only one other text of the classical period.[34] A substantial amount of information concerning the sacrifice, however, has survived in the scholia and lexica.[35]

Various explanations for the name of the sacrifice have been offered since antiquity. Some ancient commentators explained that the term derived from κοῦρος, "boy," since the sacrifice was offered on the occasion of the introduction of boys into the phratries;[36] this interpretation is unobjectionable

---

[31] Certainly this ceremony has attracted more attention from modern scholars than any other phratry ritual. For general information and bibliography consult J. Labarbe, "L'age corréspondant au sacrifice du κούρειον et les données historiques du sixième discours d'Isée," *BAB* 39 (1953), pp. 358-394; M. Golden, "Demosthenes and the Age of Majority in Athens," *Phoenix* 33 (1979), pp. 25-38; R. Sealey, *The Athenian Republic: Democracy or the Rule of Law?*, University Park 1987, pp. 13-18.

[32] Again, there is a certain amount of controversy surrounding the age at which children passsed through the sacrifice of the *koureion*. See J. Labarbe, "L'age corréspondant au sacrifice du κούρειον et les données historiques du sixième discours d'Isée," *BAB* 39 (1953), pp. 358-394. Probably the most important evidence for the age at which boys were introduced is provided by Pollux 8, 107.

[33] The evident difference in the roots of κόρειον (lines 6, 53 and 62) and κούρεον (line 118) is not a difference of Attic and Ionian dialects, as in κόρος vs. κοῦρος, but simply a difference of the grapheme for the "spurious diphthong" (see the commentary to line 114 below). For the omission of the *iota* in the suffix of κούρεον (line 118) see Threatte, *GAI* I, pp. 312, 315.

[34] Isaios 6, 21-26. Note, however, that on numerous occasions the orators describe a sacrifice which is offered when children are admitted to a phratry. Though they do not attach a specific name to this sacrifice, it is likely that it should be identified as the *koureion*. See Andocides 1, 126; [Dem.] 40, 11-15, 81-83; Isaios 7, 13-17; Isaios 8, 18-20.

[35] For a list of these citations see C.W. Hedrick, Jr., *The Attic Phratry* (Thesis, University of Pennsylvania), Ann Arbor 1984, pp. 169-174.

[36] See Schol. to Aristophanes, *Frogs*, 798; Aristophanes, *Acharnians*, 146. Inevitably they have found modern followers, *e.g.* A. Ledl, "Das attische Bürgerrecht und die Frauen," *WS* 29 (1907), p. 223. For a further review of authors who have espoused this interpretation, consult J. Labarbe, "L'age corréspondant au sacrifice du κούρειον et les données historiques du sixième discours d'Isée," *BAB* 39 (1953), p. 359 note 1.

on linguistic grounds.[37] Nevertheless, in recent years most scholars have deserted the ancients in favor of a derivation from κείρω, "to shear."[38]

The ceremony of the *koureion*, then, would be the "shearing sacrifice."[39] In some later accounts it is stated that when a candidate was introduced to a phratry he shaved his head and dedicated the hair to Artemis.[40] The importance of "shearing" as a rite of passage is, of course, well documented in ancient Greece and in many other cultures.[41]

No source explicitly states what animal was normally sacrificed at the *koureion*. It is possible that, as in the case of the *meion*, the victim may have been a goat or a sheep.[42] From the victim at the *koureion* the priest received as his dues the usual flank and haunch, as well as an ear, just as he did from the *meion* (see the commentary to lines 5-6 above). In addition he was given a broad flat cake[43] and a half-*chous* of wine.

---

[37] At one point the objection was tendered that κούρεον is not the appropriate form in Attic Greek for a word deriving from κόρος, "boy": the form should be κόρειον; see O. Müller, "Untersuchungen zur Geschichte des attische Bürger- und Eherechts," *Jahrbücher für Classischen Philologie*, supplementband 25 (1899), p. 758. As A. Ledl, "Das attische Bürgerrecht und die Frauen," *WS* 29 (1907), pp. 213-214, and others have remarked, however, the word Apatouria is itself an Ionian word, and it may easily be argued that κούρεον is also a loan word from the Ionian.

[38] The decisive point was made by K. Latte, *RE* 20, 1 (1941), phratrie, col. 752, who noticed that in an inscription of Thebes of Mykale the term κούρειον was used to describe a sacrifice offered to Hermes Κτηνίτης, "Hermes the Herd God": see Sokolowski, *LSA* no. 39, line 12. In this case the word κούρειον clearly derives from κείρω: the sacrifice was to be made at shearing time by the local shepherds.

[39] J. Labarbe, "L'age correspondant au sacrifice du κούρειον et les données historiques du sixième discours d'Isée," *BAB* 39 (1953), pp. 366-367.

[40] Hesychios *s.v.* Κουρεῶτις; Suda *s.v.* Κουρεῶτις.

[41] The anthropological comparanda are perhaps the chief reason that the derivation of the word from κείρω is preferred to that from κοῦρος. Generally on the connection between rites of passage and haircuts, see the classic anthropological discussion of A. Van Gennep, *The Rites of Passage*, 1909 (trans. M. Vizedom and G. Caffee, reprint Chicago 1960), pp. 166-167, and the remarks of the psychologist B. Bettelheim, *Symbolic Wounds: Puberty and the Envious Male*, New York 1962, p. 126. For further discussion and bibliography consult J. Labarbe, "L'age correspondant au sacrifice du κούρειον et les données historiques du sixième discours d'Isée," *BAB* 39 (1953), pp. 366-369 and P. Vidal-Naquet, "The Black Hunter," in *The Black Hunter: Forms of Thought and Forms of Society in the Greek World*, trans. A. Szegedy-Maszak, Baltimore 1986.

[42] Compare the reference of Pollux 3, 52 to ὅις φράτηρ, φράτριος αἴξ. Note further that in the case of the *koureion* offered to Hermes Κτηνίτης at Thebes of Mykale (Sokolowski, *LSA* no. 39, line 12) a young kid (ἔριφος) was a victim.

[43] For the term ἐλατήρ see Aristophanes, *Knights*, 1181 with scholium; Suda *s.v.*; Athenaios 2, 57a; Hesychios *s.v.* Compare Sokolowski, *LSCG* no. 19; Prott-Ziehen, *LGS* II, no. 17 p. 70.

The reference to wine among the priestly perquisites is tantalizing. Certainly in many sacrifices wine is normally provided as part of the ἱερεώσυνα.[44] A special phratry ceremony, the οἰνιστήρια, evidently took place in connection with the *koureion*: at the phratry ceremony in which young men cut their hair, a libation was poured to Herakles.[45] It is possible, then (though not necessary), that the wine mentioned here has some connection with this special rite.

The priestly perquisites which derive from the *meion* and the *koureion* are very similar. In both cases the priest receives ham, thighs and ear from the victim as part of his dues. Nevertheless, the greater value of the dues derived from the *koureion* would seem to imply that it was a more important rite than the *meion*. The relative importance of each sacrifice is clearest in the amounts of money allotted to the priest: from the *meion* he receives only three obols, but from the *koureion* he receives a full drachma.

SECTION 4: THE PREAMBLE

This inscription uses official state formulae to a startling degree.[46] These formulae are most obvious here, in the preamble of the inscription.

Line 9: The expression used to describe the decree of the phratry is commonly used in this and other phratry-decrees (compare below, line 114).[47] The formula patently derives from the formal decrees of the Athenian state: ἔδοξεν τῶι δημῶι. Just as the generic δῆμος is used as the equivalent of the demotic᾽ Ἀθηναῖοι to denote the constituency which passed the decree, so the generic φράτερες is used here in place of the specific name of the phratry.[48] Among phratries the one attested variant on the formula comes from a document of the phratry of the Dyaleis, where the specific name of the issuing body is used: δεδόχθαι Δυαλεῦσι.[49]

---

[44] See Sokolowski, *LSCG* no. 20, line B 50.

[45] For this practice see in particular Pollux 3, 51-3 and 6, 22. See further C.W. Hedrick, Jr., *The Attic Phratry* (Thesis, University of Pennsylvania), Ann Arbor 1984, p. 176.

[46] See W. Larfeld, *Handbuch der griechischen Epigraphie* I, Leipzig 1898, p. 825 a.

[47] See *SEG* 3, 121, line 11, re-edited now by C.W. Hedrick, Jr., "The Phratry from Paiania," *CQ* 59 (1989), 126-135; *IG* II^2 1238, line 1, re-edited now by C.W. Hedrick, Jr., "An Honorific Phratry Inscription," *AJP* 109 (1988), pp. 111-117.

[48] Compare *SIG*^{3} 921 note 8.

[49] *IG* II^2 1241, line 1.

The use of the word τάδε in this formula is curious. A demonstrative is added to the formula of the decree in only two official Attic inscriptions. In both these instances, its appearance is thought to be an archaism.[50]

Lines 9-12: The archon year provided here fixes the date of the first five sections of this inscription (see below, lines 65-68). Phormion was archon in Athens in the year 396/5.[51]

The dating formula used in the inscription is unparalleled. Most Attic phratry decrees are dated by the official Athenian archon year,[52] or are not dated at all.[53] No other phratry decree is dated by "phratriarch year."

As the name implies, the phratriarch was the chief official of the phratry. Some phratries had only one phratriarch;[54] others might have more.[55] The phratriarch was elected[56] and held office for an annual term.[57]

The functions of the phratriarch are best known from this inscription.[58] He might be charged to post notices (line 121). He presided at phratry meetings and had the power of deciding whether or not the phratry might vote on a question; when the phratry voted he distributed the ballots (lines 45-48, 79-80).[59] In conjunction with the phratry priest he administered oaths (line 35) and collected fines (lines 25-26). He also had a joint responsibility with the priest for the phratry registers (line 19).

---

[50] *IG* I³ 4, B 26: ταῦτα ἔδοξεν; *IG* I³ 105, 34: τάδε ἔδοξεν. Compare Gärtringen's commentary to IG II² 114 and P.J. Rhodes, *The Athenian Boule*, Oxford 1972, pp. 196-197.

[51] Only one citation mentions the year of his archonship: Diodoros 14, 54. See *PA* no. 14949 and J. Kirchner, *RE* 21, 1 (1941), Phormion no. 3, col. 537.

[52] *IG* II² 1241, line 30.

[53] *SEG* 3, 121; *IG* II² 1238.

[54] As is the case here, in the present inscription. Compare *IG* II² 1239; Dem. 57, 23-25.

[55] The Dyaleis had two: *IG* II² 1241, lines 5-7. The Therrikleidai had more than one: C. W. Hedrick, Jr., "Old and New on the Attic Phratry of the Therrikleidai," *Hesperia* 52 (1983), pp. 299-302.

[56] See Dem. 57, 23-25.

[57] This generalization has been deduced from the fact that the present document is dated by "phratriarch year." See K. Latte, *RE* 20, 1 (1941), φρατρίαρχος, col. 745.

[58] Generally on the office see K. Latte, *RE* 20, 1 (1941), φρατρίαρχος, cols. 745-746; Wilamowitz, *AuA* II, p. 275; C.W. Hedrick, Jr., *The Attic Phratry* (Thesis, University of Pennsylvania), Ann Arbor 1984, pp. 139-141. The office is often mentioned in contemporary inscriptions and in the speeches of the fourth-century orators. The later scholiasts and lexicographers provide little useful supplemental information: see for example the *Etymologicum Magnum s.v.* φράτορες; Harp. *s.v.* φράτερες; Suda *s.v.* φράτερες.

[59] See C.W. Hedrick, Jr., "Old and New on the Attic Phratry of the Therrikleidai," *Hesperia* 52 (1983), pp. 299-302.

Other functions are attested in other phratry inscriptions.   The phratriarch was commonly charged to erect decrees.[60] When a phratry leased or sold property, the phratriarch might supervise the transaction:[61] he would collect rent and prosecute those in arrears.[62] He might also inspect phratry property to guard it from damage by irresponsible lessees.[63]

The phratriarch mentioned here, Pantakles from Oion (*PA* 11594), is known only from these decrees. The inscription does not specify whether he came from Oion Dekeleikon or Oion Kerameikon;   the former is overwhelmingly the more likely.[64]

Prominent members of phratries usually were affiliated with demes in the vicinity of the phratry seat.[65] Thus, for example, the twin phratriarchs of the Dyaleis both came from the deme of Myrrhinous, which was also the seat of their phratry. The Demotionidai had their administrative and religious center at Dekeleia (see lines 16, 29, 53-6, 64, 76, 83, 86). Of the five phratry members mentioned in the document, two (Theodoros, line 2, and Nikodemos, line 68) are certainly members of the deme of Dekeleia. Only the phratriarch, Pantakles, was certainly not a member of this deme. Nevertheless he came from a village which had strong geographic, traditional and political ties with Dekeleia.[66]

SECTION 5: THE DECREE OF HIEROKLES

Line 13: Nothing is known of the proposer of the decree, Hierokles (*PA* 7476), beyond his proper name: his demotic is unattested. It is likely, however, that he was a member of the deme in which the phratry seat was

---

[60] *IG* II^2 1241, lines 55-56; *IG* II^2 1239, lines 24-26; *IG* II^2 1240, lines 10-11.

[61] *IG* II^2 1241, lines 5-7, 45-47.

[62] *IG* II^2 1241, lines 27-28, 36-37.

[63] *IG* II^2 1241, lines 18-20.

[64] Note, however, that though the name Pantakles is fairly common in Attica, this would be its only attestation in the deme of Oion Dekeleikon.

[65] For justification of this statement, see C.W. Hedrick, Jr., "The Phratry Shrines of Attica and Athens," *Hesperia*, forthcoming.

[66] In pre-Kleisthenic times Oion probably had little political significance apart from Dekeleia, which, as one of the "original twelve kingdoms of Attica" (*FGrHist* 328 [Philochoros] F. 94) must have dominated the neighboring regions in earliest times. After the Kleisthenic reforms, Oion was part of the same *trittys* as Dekeleia.

located (see above, commentary to lines 9-12), Dekeleia. If so, he is the only attested bearer of his name from that deme.

Lines 13-14: In the context of these decrees, the term διαδικασία designates the procedure by which applicants to the phratry are screened. This procedure is invoked in two separate situations: the "regular" scrutiny of prospective phratry members (described chiefly in the decree of Nikodemos: see lines 26, 70, 79, 94) and the "extraordinary," retroactive scrutiny of those members of the phratry who "have not yet undergone the scrutiny" (described chiefly in the decree of Hierokles: see lines 13, 15, 47).

Since the same term is used to describe the scrutiny in both cases, it is, *prima facie*, likely that substantially the same procedure was used in either circumstance. Comparison of the procedures of the "extraordinary" scrutiny with those of the "regular" scrutiny confirms this impression.[67] The two procedures would naturally be identical since the point of the retroactive scrutiny is merely to see to it that those members of the phratry who have "not yet undergone the scrutiny do so" (lines 13, 47). Thus in line 26 Hierokles, having provided for the institution of the retroactive scrutiny, tries to prevent the recurrence of the same problem by requiring that "in the future the scrutiny take place in the year following the sacrifice of the *koureion*."

It is interesting that the term διαδικασία is used to describe the examination of prospective phratry members. The verb διαδικάζω is often used technically to describe legal cases where rights (for example, inheritances, property disputes, division of property of a defaulting debtor) or obligations (for example, liturgies) are at issue.[68] In such cases there would be neither prosecutor nor defendant, but simple adjudication between contestants. The procedure described here, however, corresponds to no attested parallel. Most students of Athenian law therefore maintain that the word is not used

---

[67] See the discussion below in Chapter 4.

[68] G. Leist, *Der attische Eigentümerstreit im system der Diadikasien* (Tübinger Inaugural-dissertation), Jena 1886; J.H. Lipsius, *Das attische Recht und Rechtsverfahren* I, Leipzig 1905, pp. 463-467; A.R.W. Harrison, *The Law of Athens* I, Oxford 1968, pp. 214-217.

technically in this document,[69] but generally, as a neutral expression for "judgement."[70]

Recently it has been argued that the term διαδικασία was sometimes used to describe the trials which determined the status of the individual within the state.[71] By this definition the procedure described in the Decrees of the Demotionidai might technically be described as a διαδικασία, since membership in a phratry ultimately determines the status of the citizen within the state.[72] Unfortunately there are no satisfactory parallels for such a use of the term.[73]

The retroactive scrutiny of phratry members described in the decree of Hierokles bears some obvious similarities to the procedure of διαψήφισις or revision of deme registers. Some scholars have even suggested that the two procedures were identical, and that the term διαδικασία was used by the phratry because the more precise term, διαψήφισις had taken on a technical meaning and could describe only revisions of *deme* registers.[74] In support of their position they argue that, by a slip, διαψηφίζομαι appears in line 83 in place of διαδικάζω.[75]

This position is untenable. The retroactive διαδικασία is not the phratry equivalent of the deme διαψήφισις. The διαψήφισις was a complete review

---

[69] E. Caillemer, "Διαδικασία," in D-S 2, 1 (1892), p. 122; J.H. Lipsius, "Die Phratrie der Demotionidai," *Leipziger Studien* 16 (1894), p. 165; A.R.W. Harrison, *The Law of Athens* II, Oxford 1971, p. 36 note 3. G. Leist, *Der attische Eigentümerstreit im System der Diadikasien* (Tübinger Inauguraldissertation), Jena 1886, pp. 25-27, writing before the decipherment of side B of the *stele*, suggested that the term διαδικασία was used technically here to refer to the procedure following an appeal, ἔφεσις. Now that the decree of Nikodemos can be read, his interpretation must be discarded. See Lipsius, *art. cit.*, p. 165 note 2.

[70] For this sense of the word see P. Chantraine, *Dictionnaire étymologique de la langue grècque, histoire des mots*, Paris 1968-1980, *s.v.* δίκη; G. Thür, "Kannte das altgriechische Recht die Eigentumsdiadikasie?" *Symposion 1977. Vorträge zur griechischen und hellenistischen Rechtsdienst (Akten der Gesellschaft für griechische und hellenistische Rechtsgeschichte)*, Köln 1982, p. 56.

[71] Thür, *op. cit.*, p. 68: "(die *Diadikasia*) dient...einerseits der öffentlichen Kontrolle von Staatsrechten und sichert in anderen Fällen den Freiheitsraum der Bürgers vor staatlicher Ergriffen in sein Vermögen."

[72] *Ibid.*, p. 60.

[73] The closest parallels offered by Thür are cases involving rival claimants for an inheritance. Furthermore, Thür makes no attempt to explain why some very similar procedures (such as the introduction of 18 year olds to the deme, the δοκιμασία) are not also described by the same term.

[74] For example *RIJG* II, no. 29 p. 210.

[75] See *SIG*³ 921 note 11 and *RIJG* II, no. 29 p. 210.

of the deme registers with a vote on each demesman;[76] the retroactive διαδικασία requires *only* "those who have not yet undergone the regular διαδικασία" to do so. Furthermore the verb διαψηφίζομαι in line 83 does not refer to the retroactive διαδικασία (or, for that matter, to the revision of deme registers --see the commentary to line 83): there the word refers to the vote of the *thiasotai* in a procedure preliminary to the regular διαδικασία.

The traditional notion of a retroactive scrutiny has recently been challenged by W. Thompson.[77] He argues that the phrase ὁπόσοι μήπω διεδικάσθησαν κατὰ τὸν νόμον τὸν Δημοτιωνιδῶν (lines 13-15) does not refer to those who have somehow avoided the διαδικασία, but rather to those who are not members of the Demotionidai and so are not subject to their law, or νόμος. Since Thompson accepts Wade-Gery's thesis[78] that the Δεκελειεῖς are the phratry and the Demotionidai a *genos*, it follows that this phrase "is simply a way of saying non-gennetai."[79] He goes on to argue that "since we now hold that the Demotionidai are merely a part of the phratry and that their νόμος cannot be applied to all candidates for admission to the phratry, we cannot accept this portion of Hierokles' decree as proving that some people had been admitted to the phratry without being examined."[80] He concludes then that this phrase shows that the "phratry of the Dekeleieis" voted to hold a διαψήφισις of the entire phratry rolls "with the proviso that the genos of the Demotionidai be allowed to determine its own membership."[81]

The chief problem with Thompson's interpretation is that it does violence to the Greek of lines 13-15.[82] To begin with, the word μήπω does not conform to his reading of the line. Surely "those who have not *yet* been judged according to the law of the Demotionidai" are not the same as "those

---

[76] Dem. 57, 9-13. See now D. Whitehead, *The Demes of Attica, 508/7-ca. 250 B.C.: A Political and Social Study*, Princeton 1986, pp. 96-109; B. Haussoullier, *La vie municipale en Attique; essai sur l'organisation des dèmes au quatrième siècle* (*Librairie des écoles françaises d'Athènes et de Rome*), Paris 1884, pp. 40-42; P.J. Rhodes, *A Commentary on the Aristotelian Athenaion Politeia*, Oxford 1981, p. 188; *FGrHist* 328 (Philochoros) F. 119 with Jacoby's commentary; W.E. Thompson, "An Interpretation of the 'Demotionid' Decrees," *SO* 62 (1968), pp. 58-60.

[77] W.E. Thompson, "An Interpretation of the 'Demotionid' Decrees," *SO* 62 (1968), pp. 51-68.

[78] Wade-Gery, *Demotionidai*, discussed at length below, Chapter 4.

[79] Thompson, *art. cit.*, p. 55.

[80] Thompson, *art. cit.*, p. 57.

[81] Thompson, *art. cit.*, p. 60.

[82] I defer to the next chapter the question of the validity of Wade-Gery's identification of Demotionidai and Dekeleieis, on which all of Thompson's argument depends.

who *are* not or *cannot* be judged" by that law. In such a context, the tense of διεδικάσθησαν presents similar difficulties. The aorist does not convey the sense of a general rule, which is required for Thompson's interpretation; for that we should expect the present.[83] For Thompson's arguments to be acceptable, lines 13-15 should read ὁπόσοι μὴ διαδικάζονται κατὰ τὸν νόμον.

Line 14: This group,[84] the Demotionidai, is mentioned at two other places in the inscription (lines 21 and 30-31). The eponym of the Demotionidai is attested in one passage, a list of the children who accompanied Theseus on his voyage to Crete, preserved by Servius in his commentary to the *Aeneid*.[85] According to the manuscripts, one of the young men sent to Minos was named *Demolion Cydani*. Wilamowitz recognized the name through the corrupt Latin and rendered it in Greek as Δημοτίων Κύδαντος.[86] If Wilamowitz was right in understanding Cydani as Κύδαντος then the mythical father of Demotion was the eponym of the small deme Kydantidai, which was probably situated near the eastern coast of Attica.[87] What connection, if any, should be drawn between the Demotionidai in Dekeleia and the deme of Kydantidai is unclear.

The name Demotion is an unexceptionable Greek formation, meaning "honored among the people." It is not an uncommon name, though it seems to be attested only in Attica.[88] The name of the group is patronymic in form, as are the names of many phratries and γένη.

As appears here, the Demotionidai had their own νόμοι, laws. From the time of Solon, phratries and other ἑταιρίαι were free to formulate their own laws, insofar as they did not conflict with the laws of the Athenian state.[89]

---

[83] Or, even better, a subjunctive. See, *e.g.*, Smyth, *GG*, no. 2562. The "gnomic aorist" is not relevant to the present discussion.

[84] The identification of this group is controversial. I regard it as a phratry. For a full argument of my view, and a summary of others, see Chapter 4.

[85] Servius, commentary to the *Aeneid*, 6, 21.

[86] Wilamowitz, *AuA* II, pp. 278-279.

[87] Traill, *POA*, p. 41 note 12.

[88] No pattern emerges from the geographic distribution of the demotics of the bearers of the name. See Diodoros 11, 60; Xenophon, *Hellenika* 7, 4, 4; Hyperides 3, 31; Timokles F. 9 Kock; *IG* XII, 9, 1242, lines 14 and 16 (from the deme of Acharnai); *IG* II² 2625 (from the deme of Phegous); *SEG* 18, 36 a, line 189 = *Hesperia* 28 (1959), p. 208 face A, line 189 (from the deme of Phrearre); *SEG* 24, 162, line 62 = *Hesperia* 37 (1968), pp. 1-24, line 62 (from the deme of Prospalta).

[89] *Digest* 47, 22, 4 = E. Ruschenbusch, ΣΟΛΩΝΟΣ ΝΟΜΟΙ (*Historia Einzelschrift*, heft 9), Wiesbaden 1966, F. 76 a. See Busolt-Swoboda, *Griechische Staatskunde I*, p. 193. For the laws of the various Attic phratries see Isaios 3, 73-76; Isaios 7, 13-17; Isaios 8, 18-20.

Lines 17-18: The ritual act of voting with ballots which have lain on an altar is here expressed with a formulaic phrase (compare lines 24 and 104).[90] The custom had the effect of sanctifying or solemnizing the vote.[91]

The importance of the altar to this phratry should be apparent from a casual reading of the inscription. In the case of a vote, the *phrateres* are to take their ballots from the altar (lines 18, 29, 104). Witnesses are to swear holding on to the altar (line 76). Above all, there is an insistence that the phratry rites, that is the introduction of children, take place "at the altar at Dekeleia" (lines 54 and 67).

Other known phratry altars are consecrated both to Zeus Phratrios and to Athena Phratria.[92] It is likely that the altar of the Demotionidai was consecrated only to the most prominent god of the phratry, Zeus Phratrios. The *stele*, which was erected before the altar (lines 66-67), bears the name of that god alone at its head (see line 1 with commentary).

Lines 18-19: Here, as in other documents relating to phratry admissions, the verb εἰσάγω is used to describe the introduction of the candidate to the phratry (lines 22, 70, 95, 108, 109, 115). The concept of "introducer" is expressed by the active voice of the verb.[93] There is no distinct word for "candidate." The passive voice of the verb is used to refer to those who are introduced.[94] The use of the aorist forms of εἰσάγω has no technical significance; as used here, the tense is strictly temporal in sense.[95]

---

[90] For the phrase see Dem. 18, 134; Plutarch, *Themistokles* 17; *Perikles* 32. See also W. Mare, *A Study of the Greek ΒΩΜΟΣ in Classical Greek Literature* (Thesis, University of Pennsylvania), Philadelphia 1961, pp. 170-171.

[91] E. Reisch, *RE* 1, 2 (1894), Altar, col. 1690; Mare, *op. cit.* p. 170. The latter includes a discussion of the voting practices in phratries which is vitiated by his exclusion of the epigraphical evidence from consideration.

[92] Two Attic phratry altars have been preserved, both of which were consecrated to Zeus and Athena Phratrios: H.A. Thompson, "Buildings on the West Side of the Agora," *Hesperia* 6 (1937), pp. 104-107; N. Kyparissis and H.A. Thompson, "A Sanctuary of Zeus and Athena Phratrios Newly Found in Athens," *Hesperia* 7 (1938), pp. 615-619; C.W. Hedrick, Jr., "The Temple and Cult of Apollo Patroos in Athens," *AJA* 92 (1988), pp. 185-210. One other phratry seems to have had an altar devoted only to Zeus Phratrios: Dem. 43, 11-15, 81-83. There are also references to phratry altars at Aesch. 2, 147; Andocides 1, 126; Isaios 7, 13-17.

[93] See below, lines 95 and 109; Dem. 39, 20-21; [Dem.] 59, 13, 55, 118; Isaios 7, 13-17; Isaios 2, 14-17; Isaios 8, 18-20.

[94] As here, line 19, and below, lines 83, 117; Dem. 39, 29-30; [Dem.] 43, 11-15, 81-83; [Dem.] 44, 41; Dem. 57, 43; [Dem.] 59, 59; Isaios 6, 10-11; Isaios 10, 8-9, 15, 21; P. Oxy. 31, 2538, col. 3, lines 2-3.

[95] As here, line 19, and below, line 22. See further the discussion in Chapter 4; Dem. 39, 4, 29-30; Dem. 40, 11; Dem. 43, 11-15; Dem. 57, 46, 67-69; Isaios 3, 73-76, 79-80; Isaios 6, 10-11; Isaios 10, 15; P. Oxy. 31, 2538, col. 2, lines 23-28, col. 3, lines 2-3.

Lines 20-22: As we see here, the Demotionidai kept a duplicate set of the records of their membership.[96] The original copies were kept in the archives, in the group's sanctuary;[97] where the copy[98] was kept is unknown. In line 97 the plural, τὰ κοινὰ γραμματεῖα, refers to both the copy and original.[99]

The priest and phratriarch clearly share the responsibility for the phratry's archives, since both are charged to erase offending names "from the archive and the copy." It is not certain, however, whether they share the responsibility for both lists equally, or whether each was charged with the keeping of one register.[100] In either case, the shared supervision of the registers by two officials increases security.

Line 22: Scholars who have dealt generally with the term ἀποδικάζω have been unanimous in giving it the unqualified definition "to acquit (a defendant)," or "to throw a case out of court."[101] Commentators on this inscription, however, have uniformly translated the participle ἀποδικασθέντα here as "the person rejected,"[102] the polar opposite of the dictionary definition

---

[96] Phratry registers are also mentioned at [Dem.] 44, 4; Isaios 7, 13-17 and 26-27; Suda *s.v.* Ἀπατούρια.

[97] The term γραμματεῖον has been treated by A. Wilhelm, *Beiträge zur griechischen Inschriftenkunde* (*Sonderschriften des OeAI in Wien*, bd. 7), Vienna 1909, pp. 229-299 and G. Klaffenbach, *Bemerkungen zum griechischen Urkundenwesen* (*SDAW* no. 6), Berlin 1960, though both these scholars are concerned chiefly with official state records. The term γραμματεῖον means "archives" (not a specific list) and is on occasion used to denote the building in which the archives are kept: see Wilhelm, *op. cit.*, p. 255. The ellipse in the phrase ἐν Δημοτιωνιδῶν is explained by Schwyzer, *GG* II, p. 120 note 2. We may presume the omission of some word such as ἱερόν or οἰκία.

[98] For the word ἀντίγραφον see Klaffenbach, *op. cit.*, pp. 38-42.

[99] See *SIG*³ 921 note 15; Wilhelm, *op. cit.*, p. 248.

[100] See below, lines 121-125, where the phratriarch is to post an announcement in the city, the priest in the sanctuary of Leto.

[101] See Stephanos, *Thesauros, s.v.*; Preisigke, *Wörterbuch, s.v.*; Preisigke, *Fachwörterbuch, s.v.*; *LSJ, s.v.*; H. Frisk, *Griechisches etymologisches Wörterbuch*, Heidelberg 1960-70, *s.v.*; P. Chantraine, *Dictionnaire étymologique de la langue grècque, histoire des mots*, Paris 1968-1980, *s.v.*; B. Bérard, *De arbitrio inter liberas graecorum civitates*, Paris 1894; A. Wilhelm, "Zu griechischen Inschriften," *AEMOe* 20 (1897), p. 80 note 34; J.H. Lipsius, *Das attische Recht und Rechtsverfahren*, Leipzig 1905-1915, p. 959 note 13; Graeca Halensis, *Dikaiomata*, Berlin 1913, pp. 59-60; O. Gradenwitz, *Zum Falscheid des P. Halensis 1 (Dikaiomata)*, (*SHAW* 6, no. 8), Heidelberg 1913, p. 16 note 8.

[102] This translation is tacitly based on context: ἀποδικάζω is taken as a reference to the rejection described in the lines immediately preceding. Most scholars make no attempt to justify their translation: see F.B. Tarbell, "The Decrees of the Demotionidai, a Study of the Attic Phratry," *Papers of the American School in Athens* 5 (1886-1890), p. 176; Wilamowitz, *AuA* II, p. 260; *RIJG* II, no. 29 p. 201; Wade-Gery, *Demotionidai*, p. 120. Those who note the discrepancy between their translation and the dictionary definition of the term generally

of the word. Furthermore, there has so far been no attempt to explain why ἀποδικάζω is used at this point and this point alone in the document. If Hierokles simply wanted to express the notion of "to reject" he might just as well have used some form of the verb ἀποψηφίζομαι, as indeed both he and Nikodemos regularly do throughout their respective decrees (see below, commentary to line 31). In fact, if the participle here simply refers to rejection, it could have been omitted without damage to the clarity of the passage: the cause of the fine imposed on the introducer is perfectly clear from the lines preceding.

For the reader's convenience, it may be useful at this point to quote the most important attestations of the verb:[103]

1) *IC* IV, 22b (VII/VI B.C.): πρόθεσιν μήτ᾽ ἀ[πο]δικάζαι μήτ᾽ ἀπ-ομ[όσαι]

2) Antiphon 6, 47: οἵτινες ἅπερ αὐτοὶ σφᾶς αὐτοὺς οὐκ ἔπεισαν, ταῦθ᾽ ὑμᾶς ἀξιοῦσι πεῖσαι, καὶ ἃ αὐτοὶ ἔργῳ ἀπεδίκασαν, ταῦθ᾽ ὑμᾶς κελεύουσι καταδικάσαι.

3) Kritias F. 71 D (*apud* Pollux 8, 25): Κριτίας δὲ ἀποδικάσαι ἔφη τὴν δίκην τὸ ἀπολῦσαι ἢ νικῶσαν ἀποφῆναι ὡς ἂν ἡμεῖς ἀποψηφίσασθαι. ὁ δὲ αὐτὸς καὶ διαδικάζειν τὸ δι᾽ ὅλου τοῦ ἔτους δικάζειν.

4) Aristotle, *Politics*, 1268 B, 2, 9: ἔτι δ᾽ οὐδεὶς ἐπιορκεῖν ἀναγκάζει τὸν ἁπλῶς ἀποδικάσαντα ἢ καταδικάσαντα, εἴπερ ἁπλῶς τὸ ἔγκλημα γέγραπται, δικαίως· οὐ γὰρ μηδὲν ὀφείλειν ὁ ἀποδικάσας κρίνει ἀλλὰ τὰς εἴκοσι μνᾶς· ἀλλ᾽ ἐκεῖνος ἤδη ἐπιορκεῖ ὁ καταδικάσας μὴ νομίζων ὀφείλειν τὰς εἴκοσι μνᾶς.

5) *SIG*³ 953, lines 83-85 (Kalymna, II B.C.): ἀπεδικάσθη παρόν-των· τᾶν ψάφων ταὶ καταδικάζουσαι ἑβδομήκοντα ὀκτώ, ταὶ δὲ ἀποδικάζουσαι ἑκατὸν ἴκατι ἕξ.

---

maintain that the term is used here as the equivalent of ἀποψηφίζομαι: ꜱee J.H. Lipsius, "Die Phratrie der Demotionidai," *Leipziger Studien* 16 (1894), p. 168, and *SIG*³ 921 note 11. There are of course parallels for the use of ἀποψηφίζομαι with such varied meanings as "reject," "acquit" and "vote the franchise away": see, *e.g.*, *LSJ s.v.* No such parallel exists for ἀποδικάζω.

[103] I limit discussion here to the verb. The adjective ἀπόδικος carries the same meaning as the verb, but is passive in sense: ἡ ἀπόδικος πόλις means "the city which has been acquitted," or "the city which has had the charges against it dismissed." The word is used most frequently in the context of international arbitration. See generally B. Bérard, *De arbitrio inter liberas graecorum civitates*, Paris 1894.

6) P. Hal. 1, lines 55-63 (III B.C.): ἐὰν δὲ ἀποδ[ικ]ασθείσης
αὐτῶι [δί]κης ἐπιλάβηται τῶν μα[ρ]τύρων καὶ γραψάμενος
δίκην ψευδομαρ[τ]υρίου νικήσηι, οἵ [τ]ε μαρτύρης τὴν
καταδίκην εἰσπρασσέσ[θ]ωσαν κατὰ τὸ διάγραμμα καὶ ὁ
παρασχόμ[ε]νος αὐτοὺς ἀποτινέτω τῶι νικήσαντι τό τε
τίμημα τῆς ἀποδικα[σ]θείσης δίκης, ἐφ' ἧς παρέσχετο τοὺς
μάρτυρας, [κ]αὶ τὸ ἐπιδέκατον ἢ ἐπιπεντεκαιδ[έ]κατον.

7) P. Petr. 21 a, lines 3 and 9 (III B.C.):
[δίκη ἔρημος ἀπεδικάσθη ἣν ἐγρά]ψατ[ο] Πυθίων.
δίκη ἔρημος ἀπεδικάσ[θη ἣ]ν ἐγράψα[το Πυθίων].

8) P. Gurob. 2, line 49 (III B.C.): [κρινέ]τωσαν ἀδικῆσαι. ἀπ-
εδικάσεμεν τὴ[ν δίκην].

9) Polyainos 3, 9, 15: Ἰφικράτης θανάτου δίκην φεύγων παρ-
εστήσατο νεανίσκους ἐγχειρίδια κατέχοντας, οἳ
παραφαίνοντες τοῖς δικασταῖς τὰς λαβὰς οὕτως αὐτοὺς
κατέπληξαι ὥστε φοβηθέντες ἀπεδίκασαν τὴν δίκην.

10) Pollux 8, 9: καὶ τὸ ἔργον αὐτοῦ (i.e. τοῦ δικαστοῦ) θέσθαι τὴν
ψῆφον ἐξενεγκεῖν γνῶσιν, κρῖναι διακρῖναι τὰ δίκαια,
διελεῖν, δικάσαι καταδικάσαι ἀποδικάσαι, καταψηφίσασθαι
ἀποψηφίσασθαι, καταγνῶναι ἀπογνῶναι, τιμωρήσασθαι
κολάσαι μετελθεῖν, ἀφεῖναι ἀπαλλάξαι.

11) Diogenes Laertius 1 (Chilon) 71: κρίνων γάρ ποτε φίλῳ δίκην
αὐτὸς μὲν κατὰ τὸν νόμον, τὸν δὲ φίλον πείσειεν ἀποδικάσαι
αὐτοῦ, ἵνα ἀμφότερα καὶ τὸν νόμον καὶ τὸν φίλον τηρήσαι.

12) Argument to Aristophanes, Wasps, 15-17: καὶ δύο κύνες ἐπ-
εισάγονται πολιτικῶς παρ' αὐτῷ κρινόμενοι· καὶ κατὰ τοῦ
φεύγοντος ἐκφέρειν συνεχῶς τὴν ψῆφον μέλλων ἀπατηθεὶς
ἄκων τὴν ἀποδικάζουσαν φέρει τὴν ψῆφον.

From these passages it should be clear that the meaning of the verb is
indeed "to acquit," or "to dismiss a case from court." The egregious
exception is number 1, where it must mean something like "avoid a duty by
means of a court decision."[104]

As important as the contextual meaning of the verb in these passages is
the syntactical construction which it takes. Normally the object of the verb is
δίκη (numbers 3, 6, 7, 8, 9). The person acquitted is in the genitive (numbers

---

[104] I follow M. Guarducci, commentary to IC IV, 22b: "significans qui vel judicio vel
sacramento aliquid a se arcere conetur."

5, 11)[105] or the dative (number 6). Again, the only exception is number 1, where the thing one wishes to avoid is the object of the verb.[106] The construction taken by the verb to some extent clarifies its precise meaning: very literally, "to dismiss a person's case from court."

All parallels contradict the usual interpretation of ἀποδικασθέντα in this inscription. Furthermore, the construction used here is also unparalleled: here it is the *person* who is the object of the verb (or actually, since the verb is passive, the subject, which amounts to the same thing).

The tense of the participle provides a neglected clue as to the meaning of the word. Elsewhere in the decree of Hierokles the aorist is used temporally, to refer to past actions of the phratry (see above, commentary to lines 18-19, and the discussion of the procedure of the "extraordinary" scrutiny below, Chapter 4). Thus in lines 18-19 the aorist infinitive ἐσαχθῆναι designates the action by which the candidate *originally* gained admission to the phratry. The aorist should not refer to a rejection in the (relatively) present scrutiny; for that the present tense would be used.

The decree of Hierokles begins by ordering that the *phrateres* immediately scrutinize "those who have not yet been scrutinized" (lines 13-18). Anyone who is found to have been introduced "though not a *phrater*" is to be ejected, his name erased from the phratry's registers (lines 18-22). The one who *originally* introduced this ἀποδικασθέντα is to pay a fine (lines 22-24). I would suggest that this participle refers not to the ejection of lines 18-22, but to the *original* condition of the candidate, as described in lines 13-18. In other words, an ἀποδικασθέντα is someone who *has not undergone the scrutiny at all*; the participle is the equivalent of the phrase τὸν μήπω διαδικασθέντα (lines 13-14).[107] The attested meaning of ἀποδικάζω, "dismiss (a case) from court," and hence not judge it, and the unusual construction with the personal object which it has taken in the present passage support the proposed interpretation: "a person whose case has been dismissed from court," that is, who has not been judged.

The expression τὸν ἀποδικασθέντα, then, probably refers to someone who has, by whatever means, managed to bypass the phratry scrutiny. The use of the passive form of a compound of δικάζω implies an action or

---

[105] See A. Wilhelm, "Zu griechischen Inschriften," *AEMOe* 20 (1897), p. 80 note 34.

[106] In number 2 the object is the neuter plural relative. I take this as a reference to an unexpressed feminine plural, δίκαι.

[107] It is a small point that ἀπό sometimes has a virtual *alpha privative* sense in compounds. See *LSJ s.v.*, D 6.

decision on the part of some legal agency to allow certain members of the phratry to bypass the scrutiny. If this is the case, then the participle explains to some extent how it happened that certain members of the phratry might "not yet be scrutinized": by some prior decision they were exempted from the scrutiny. The best known such decision is the general amnesty of 403, which exempted those born before that year from meeting the requirements of the citizenship law of Perikles (see below, commentary to line 59).

Lines 28-29: The Apatouria was the peculiar festival of the phratry in the Ionian world, celebrated in Athens each Fall in the month of Pyanopsion. At the festival new members were inducted into the phratry. The festival lasted for three days: in order, *Dorpia, Anarrusis*, and *Koureotis*.[108]

Line 30: The term ἔφεσις is well and clearly attested in Attica and elsewhere with the technical, juridical meaning, "appeal" (see lines 38 and 96). Even so, it is probably the most debated word in the entire document,[109] for the interpretation of it determines the identities of the Demotionidai and the House of the Dekeleians. I reserve discussion of it in the context of the admission procedure to the next chapter.

Line 31: The verb ἀποψηφίζομαι is used consistently throughout the Decrees of the Demotionidai to describe the rejection of a candidate (lines 31, 39, 90, 95, 98-99, 101 and 102-103). Two phrases are used to describe the acceptance of a candidate: ψηφίζονται εἶναι αὐτοῖς φράτερα (lines 88-89) and δοκεῖ εἶναι αὐτοῖς φράτερα (lines 96-97; compare lines 18 and 37). The phrases seem to be used interchangeably. Other compounds with ψηφίζομαι

---

[108] There is a substantial bibliography on the festival of the Apatouria. The following essays are of fundamental importance: J. Töpffer, *RE* 1 (1894), 'Ἀπατούρια, cols. 2672-2680; A. Mommsen, *Feste der Stadt Athen*, Leipzig 1898, pp. 323-349; S. Eitrem, "Die Labyadai und die Byzyga," *Eranos* 20 (1921-1922), pp. 91-121; L. Deubner, *Attische Feste*, Berlin 1932, pp. 232-234; J. Labarbe, "L'age corréspondant au sacrifice du κούρειον et les données historiques du sixième discours d'Isée," *BAB* 39 (1953), pp. 358-394; J.D. Mikalson, *The Sacred and Civic Calendar of the Athenian Year*, Princeton 1975, p. 79; P. Vidal-Naquet, "The Black Hunter," in *The Black Hunter: Forms of Thought and Forms of Society in the Greek World*, trans. A. Szegedy-Maszak, Baltimore 1986; *idem*, "The Black Hunter Revisited," *PCPS* 212 n.s. 32 (1986), pp. 126-144. The following may be consulted for a general introduction to the festival: M.P. Nilsson, *Cults, Myths, Oracles and Politics in Ancient Greece*, 1951 (reprint New York 1972), pp. 165-170; H.W. Parke, *Festivals of the Athenians*, London 1977, pp. 88-92. For further bibliography and discussion of specific problems see C.W. Hedrick, Jr., *The Attic Phratry* (Thesis, University of Pennsylvania), Ann Arbor 1984, pp. 153-176.

[109] The appeal in the context of the procedures of the "extraordinary" and "regular" scrutinies is discussed in Chapter 4. For general information see M. Just, *Die Ephesis in der Geschichte des attischen Prozesses-- ein Versuch zur Deutung der Rechtsnatur der Ephesis* (Thesis Würzburg), Würzburg 1965, and especially pp. 308-323, where he reviews the theories which have been advanced about the appeal in this inscription. See also A.R.W. Harrison, *The Law of Athens* II, Oxford 1971, pp. 72-74.

are used to describe the phratriarch "putting the vote" (ἐπιψηφίζομαι, lines 45-46) and to announce the verdict which the thiasotai bring in (ὁπότερ' ἂν ψηφίσωνται, lines 87-8). The process of the vote is once described by the verb διαψηφίζομαι (lines 83-84), which is commonly used of actions in which citizenship is at issue.[110]

Line 32: This passage does not describe unambiguously what precise role the συνήγοροι are to play in the proceedings of the "extraordinary" scrutiny. All we know is derived from this line and the oath which the συνήγοροι are to swear, which is cited verbatim at lines 36-37.

Wilamowitz took the συνήγοροι to be accusers. He held that a preliminary decision concerning the candidates was made in line 29 by the "House of the Dekeleians." This group then appointed συνήγοροι to prosecute those candidates who appealed their decision to the Demotionidai.[111]

Wade-Gery argued against Wilamowitz' interpretation, submitting that it was inconsistent with the oath sworn by the συνήγοροι: "it is improper for the accusers to take an oath as to what verdict they will permit."[112] He argued that the συνήγοροι were instead "assessors," citing the συνήγοροι who worked with the ten λογισταί at the εὔθυνα. These συνήγοροι, he held, "helped to conduct the enquiry and pronounce the decision: they are not briefed for the prosecution or the defence."[113] The preposition ἐπί in this passage he took to mean "in addition to." Hence, for Wade-Gery this line should be translated "a board of assessors to serve with them (*sc.* the Demotionidai)."

At Athens, συνήγοροι are attested with four functions.[114] First, as Wade-Gery alleged, we know that a board of ten συνήγοροι were selected by lot from the citizen body to serve with the λογισταί at the εὔθυνα. Evidence for their duties at these proceedings is very sparse, but it is now assumed by most scholars that they served as "public prosecutors."[115] The term

---

[110] See P.J. Rhodes, *A Commentary on the Aristotelian Athenaion Politeia*, Oxford 1981, p. 499. Compare also the use of the verb in Isaios 7, 13-17.

[111] Wilamowitz, *AuA* II, p. 260.

[112] Wade-Gery, *Demotionidai*, p. 128.

[113] *Ibid.*, p. 128 note 3.

[114] See D.M. MacDowell, ed., *Aristophanes, Wasps*, Oxford 1971, pp. 198-199; *idem, The Law in Classical Athens*, London 1978, pp. 61-62, 170-171.

[115] P.J. Rhodes, *A Commentary on the Aristotelian Athenaion Politeia*, Oxford 1981, pp. 501 and 597, with bibliography there cited. This interpretation obviously eliminates Wade-Gery's analogy.

συνήγορος was also applied to a person, usually a close friend or relative of the person on trial, who spoke on behalf of a defendant. The word might also be used to describe state appointed speakers, who, when the question of repealing a law arose, spoke on behalf of the law. Finally, it is known that in trials concerning treason, συνήγοροι were appointed to serve as "public prosecutors."[116]

It emerges, then, that there is no evidence to support Wade-Gery's interpretation of this term, but much in favor of that of Wilamowitz. It should be noted, however, that neither is Wilamowitz' interpretation certain. The συνήγορος is not by nature a speaker for either prosecution or defense. The term means literally "joint speaker": the συνήγορος spoke on behalf of the person or group who appointed him, and his function thus might involve either prosecution or defense, depending on the cirumstances of his client. So, as a basis for the definition of the συνήγοροι in the present context, it may be said that they are to speak on behalf of the House of the Dekeleians. Given the oath they swear it may also be supposed that they will speak to the issue of the admission or rejection of candidates:[117] it is most natural to suppose that they are accusers.

The phrase which describes the object of the activity of the συνήγοροι, ἐπ᾽ αὐτοῖς, is unfortunately vague. The demonstrative αὐτοῖς probably refers to the appellants, since they are the focus of the preceding clauses, and not to the Demotionidai, as Wade-Gery suggested. The meaning of the preposition ἐπί, though, is uncertain: it can be used with the dative to mean either "for" or "against." I would suggest that the latter alternative is preferable. It would have been possible (and more normal) for Hierokles to express the former idea, "speak on behalf of," by using συνηγορέω and a simple dative.[118]

Line 33:   The proper name of this corporation, "House of the Dekeleians," is not attested in any other document. The use of the word οἶκος as the title of a group is virtually unparalleled. The name Δεκελειεῖς, on the other hand, is abundantly and unambiguously attested as the demotic of the deme of Dekeleia. In the following paragraphs I examine these two

---

[116] D.M. MacDowell, *The Law in Classical Athens*, London 1978, pp. 61-62, 170-171; A.R.W. Harrison, *The Law of Athens* II, Oxford 1971, pp. 158-161.

[117] Wade-Gery's objection here seems ill-advised, for a prosecutor can easily "permit the admission of someone not qualified," simply by not doing his job as a prosecutor. See the commentary below to line 36.

[118] It is also possible that ἐπί is used to express the idea of "on the subject of," that is, "either for or against." On this interpretation the συνήγοροι are either to aid or attack the appellants on the basis of their merits.

terms. I defer discussion of the role of the group in the "extraordinary" scrutiny and its relationship to the Demotionidai to the next two chapters.

If the members of this group were simply called the Δεκελειεῖς, no one would dispute that they were the demesmen of Dekeleia: there is no indisputable evidence that the name was ever used to describe anyone other than the members of that deme.[119] The seat of the phratry was located in Dekeleia (a geographical connection which is often emphasized in this document), and many of the prominent members of this phratry were also members of that deme (see above, commentary to lines 11-12). Nevertheless, it is conceivable that some group in the vicinity of Dekeleia, such as a *genos* or phratry, might also have been called Δεκελειεῖς. The demotic form of the name is not in and of itself sufficient to rule out such a possibility. For example, some γένη are attested with demotic names such as Σαλαμίνιοι, ᾽Ικαριεῖς and Κεφισιεῖς.[120] One Attic phratry with an analogous name, the Δυαλεῖς,[121] is also known.

Many (perhaps most) scholars today would identify the Δεκελειεῖς as a *genos* or phratry. Two texts are normally cited as supporting evidence for the existence of such a group,[122] both of which seem to distinguish a group called Δεκελειεῖς from the demesmen of Dekeleia.

Herodotus, in his account of those who distinguished themselves at the battle of Plataia (9, 73) remarks:

᾽Αθηναίων δὲ λέγεται εὐδοκιμῆσαι Σωφάνης ὁ Εὐτυχίδεω ἐκ δήμου Δεκελεῆθεν, Δεκελέων δὲ τῶν κότε ἐργασαμένων ἔργον χρήσιμον ἐς τὸν πάντα χρόνον, ὡς αὐτοὶ ᾽Αθηναῖοι λέγουσι.

Of the Athenians Sophanes son of Eutychides of the deme of Dekeleia is said to have excelled, while the Dekeleians once accomplished a deed which has been useful to them for all time, as the Athenians themselves say.

---

[119] For the demotic Δεκελειεύς and the adverb Δεκελειόθεν see Steph. Byz. *s.v.* Δεκελεία; A. Milchhöfer, *RE* 4, 2 (1901), Dekeleia, col. 2425.

[120] See J. Töpffer, *Attische Genealogie*, Berlin 1889, p. 3; *RIJG* II, no. 29 p. 216.

[121] *IG* II² 1241.

[122] See R. Schöll, "Die kleisthenischen Phratrien," *SBAW* (1889), part 2, p. 19 note 1; J. Töpffer, *Attische Genealogie*, Berlin 1889, pp. 289-291; Wade-Gery, *Demotionidai*, p. 123 note 1 and the appendix, pp. 133-134; *RIJG* II, no. 29 pp. 215-217.

Herodotus then digresses to discuss this deed of the Dekeleians: in days of old Theseus abducted Helen, and the Tyndaridai reclaimed her. At a critical moment Dekelos, fearing for the country and despising Theseus' crime, took the side of the Dorians. So, Herodotus says, the Dekeleians enjoyed special honors at Sparta, and, in the early years of the Peloponnesian War, though the invader ravaged the rest of Attica, he left Dekeleia untouched.

This passage uses two expressions to describe the inhabitants of Dekeleia: those ἐκ δήμου Δεκελεῆθεν and Δεκελειεῖς. It is not clear whether these two expressions refer to distinguishable groups, or are simply variations of the same name. Those who would use this passage as evidence for a *genos* or phratry of the Δεκελειεῖς of course argue that Herodotus makes a distinction between the two.[123] On their interpretation we are asked to imagine that Herodotus, mentioning the name of Sophanes of the deme of Dekeleia, thinks of an homonymous kinship group and digresses to tell a story about them. Alternatively, it is possible, and much more likely, that the mention of the deme of Dekeleia prompts a digression about the deme.[124]

The second passage commonly cited as a witness for the *genos* of the Δεκελειεῖς comes from the orator Lysias (23, 2). Here the speaker tells how he tried to summon a certain Pankleon to court and, presuming that he was a metic, began proceedings before the Polemarch. Pankleon, however, maintained that he was a Plataian, and hence at this period in possession of full Athenian citizenship, with "deme residence" in Dekeleia:

ἐπειδὴ δὲ ἀπεκρίνατο ὅτι Δεκελειόθεν προσκαλεσάμενος αὐτὸν
καὶ πρὸς τοὺς τῇ ᾿Ιπποθωντίδι δικάζοντας, ἐλθὼν ἐπὶ τὸ κουρεῖον
τὸ παρὰ τοὺς᾿ Ἑρμᾶς, ἵνα οἱ Δεκελειεῖς προσφοιτῶσιν, ἠρώτων οὕς
τε ἐξευρίσκοιμι Δεκελειῶν ἐπυνθανόμην εἴ τινα γιγνώσκοιεν
Δεκελειόθεν δημοτευόμενον Παγκλέωνα.

---

[123]   Thus, for example, Wade-Gery claims that the use of δέ between ἐκ δήμου Δεκελειῆθεν and Δεκελειεῖς should be taken as emphasizing the contrast. As Wade-Gery himself admits, however, this might just as well be the epexegetic δέ: see Wade-Gery, *Demotionidai*, p. 133.

[124]   Certainly throughout the digression Herodotos uses Δεκελειεῖς to describe the demesmen: see 9, 73.2, where Δεκελειεῖς are clearly one of the "Thesean" δῆμοι, and especially 9, 74.1, the sentence which closes the digression on the Δεκελειεῖς: τούτου τοῦ δήμου ἐὼν ὁ Σωφάνης.

When he answered that he was from Dekeleia, I summoned him before those who judge for the tribe Hippothontis. Then I went to the barbershop near the Herms which the Dekeleians frequent, and asked any Dekeleians whom I could find whether they knew any demesman from Dekeleia named Pankleon.

Again, in this passage two expressions are used to describe the inhabitants of Dekeleia: Δεκελειεῖς and Δεκελειόθεν δημοτευόμενοι.[125] The question remains the same: do these expressions refer to different groups, or are they variations on the same name? The place described by Lysias' speaker as "frequented by the Dekeleians" is evidently the same as that mentioned in these decrees (see below, commentary to lines 63-64). Those who would use this citation as evidence for a *genos* or phratry of the Δεκελειεῖς ask us to imagine that the speaker, in order to determine the truth of Pankleon's claim that he is a member of the deme of Dekeleia, has gone to the place where the members of the phratry or *genos* of the Dekeleians congregate and has spoken to them, rather than going to talk to the members of the deme. Again, it is possible (and more likely) that the Δεκελειεῖς here mentioned are demesmen, and that the speaker is addressing his queries to those who are best qualified to answer.

The case for identifying a *genos* or phratry of the Δεκελειεῖς has been most clearly and succinctly stated by Wade-Gery: "(both demesmen and *phrateres*) are commonly and correctly called Δεκελειεῖς, but demesmen could be called more distinctively τοῦ δήμου Δεκελειόθεν or Δεκελειόθεν δημοτευόμενοι and this is done in these two passages: in our decrees on the other hand no such distinction is made since Δεκελειησ [*sic*] means phratry throughout."[126]

It should be clear that there is little evidence to recommend this position. The word Δεκελειεύς is the proper demotic of Dekeleia; Δεκελειόθεν is a simple adverb, "from Dekeleia."[127] Furthermore, as we have seen, neither Herodotus nor Lysias gives anything like unequivocal or

---

[125] Elsewhere in the text, where Pankleon is described simply as Δεκελειόθεν we should assume δημοτευόμενος. See L. Gernet and M. Bizos, eds., *Lysias*, Paris 1924-1926, commentary to Lysias 23, 2.

[126] Wade-Gery, *Demotionidai*, p. 133.

[127] Steph. Byz. *s.v.* Δεκελεία. See also A. Milchöfer, *RE* 4, 2 (1901), Dekeleia, col. 2425. The informal, periphrastic character of the adverb is clear in the citations from Herodotos and Lysias. In neither case is the adverb sufficient of itself to describe the demesmen. It must be qualified by such phrases as ἐκ δήμου and δημοτευόμενος.

unimpeachable evidence for the use of Δεκελειεῖς as the name of a *genos* or phratry. So it appears that there is no evidence for any group called Δεκελειεῖς other than the demesmen.

The other component of the name of this group, οἶκος, is well attested with the meaning "building" or "family" and the like, but as the official name of an association it is considerably rarer;[128] so rare that it was once thought to be confined to associations of seafarers from the region of the Black Sea.[129] There can be no doubt that the term is here used as the proper name of a group, since it governs verbs which describe the actions of the group.[130]

Most scholars have insisted that the term οἶκος here has connotations of kinship, as in the use of the word for "family."[131] Wilamowitz, for example, suggested a parallel from Pindar's sixth Isthmian ode.[132] The recipient of the ode, Phylakidas son of Lampon from Aegina, had won a victory in the pankration, as had other members of his immediate family. He and his relatives are said to "sprinkle with the dew of the Graces the πάτρα (a Doric approximation of the phratry) of the Psalychiadai and keeping straight the οἶκος of Themistios (probably the maternal grandfather of Phylakidas, who was also a pankratiast), they dwell in this god-beloved city."[133]

There are, of course, obvious problems in using high poetry in the Dorian dialect to explain a term from a prosaic Attic inscription. There are problems in equating an Aeginetan πάτρα with an Attic phratry. Fortunately the meaning of οἶκος in this poem is not so problematic. Pindar mentions three groups to which the athletes belong: οἶκος, πάτρα and πόλις. In this sequence, the common and well attested meaning of οἶκος, "family," is appropriate. It is, of course, common to describe a family by the name of its

---

[128] See F. Poland, *Geschichte des griechischen Vereinswesens* (*Gekrönte Preisschrift* 38), Leipzig 1909, pp. 114 and 459-464, who deals with the buildings connected with such associations; A. Wilhelm, *Beiträge zur griechischen Inschriftenkunde* (*Sonderschriften des OeAI in Wien*, bd. 7), Vienna 1909, pp. 51-52; L. Robert, *Collection Froehner*, Paris 1936, pp. 5-6, no. 8; *idem*, "Inscriptions d'Athènes et de la Grèce centrale," *ArchEph* (1966), pp. 7-14. For bibliography and discussion of the οἶκος as family, consult R. Sealey, *The Athenian Republic: Democracy or the Rule of Law?*, University Park 1987, pp. 25-27.

[129] See Poland, *op. cit.*, pp. 459-464.

[130] The word is not necessarily used of kinship groups as Wilamowitz thought: *AuA* II, p. 266. See further Andrewes, *Philochoros*, p. 4 note 14.

[131] See for example Wilamowitz, *AuA* II, p. 266: "Haus, οἶκος, ist ein gentilicischer Begriff und kann hier nicht anders gefasst werden."

[132] *Ibid.* A review of the various theories may be found in the *RIJG* II, no. 29 p. 215.

[133] Pindar, *Isthmian* 6, 63-65.

nominal head. The "family of Themistios" is scarcely an enlightening parallel for the οἶκος of the Dekeleians.

Another passage which has been cited as a parallel for the οἶκος of the Dekeleians comes from Demosthenes.[134] The speaker claims that "he introduced the boy into the phratry of Hagnias so that the οἶκος of Hagnias should not become extinct." It has been suggested that the speaker means by οἶκος a subsection of a phratry. It seems, to the contrary, perfectly clear from the context of the passage that the οἶκος mentioned here is the family of Hagnias. The phrase used in this passage, οἶκος ἐξερημωθῆναι, for example, is a cliché used to describe the circumstances of a family lacking male heirs and hence on the verge of extinction. The boy is introduced into the phratry because it is a necessary part of the procedure of adoption. This reference to the family of Hagnias explains nothing about the οἶκος of the Dekeleians.

The term οἶκος is attested as the formal name of a corporation in three inscriptions from Athens.[135] In each, the group is an association of seafarers. The name of the organization derives not from any putative ties of kinship, but from the building in which they gather to dine.[136] The corporate name οἶκος is also used in a number of inscriptions from the Black Sea. All of these date to the Imperial period, and again it seems that all take their names from the buildings in which they meet.[137] As all attested groups with the name οἶκος derive their name from their "clubhouse," the same is likely to be true of the "House" of the Dekeleians: a group of Dekeleians who meet in an οἶκος.

A variety of ancient groups met in, and hence might conceivably be called, οἶκοι. The Attic *genos* of the Kerykes, for example, evidently

---

[134] [Dem.] 43, 11-15. The suggestion has been made by W.K. Lacey, *The Family in Classical Greece*, Ithaca 1968, p. 92. His reasons for the suggestion are unclear to me.

[135] Two of the inscriptions emanate from the same group and date respectively to 112-11 B.C. and 111-10 B.C.: B.D. Meritt, "Greek Inscriptions," *Hesperia* 30 (1961), nos. 28 and 29, pp. 229-230. The third inscription dates to the end of the fourth century or the beginning of the third: L. Robert, *Collection Froehner*, Paris 1936, no. 8, pp. 5-6. The three inscriptions were edited and explicated *ensemble* by L. Robert, "Inscriptions d'Athènes et de la Grèce centrale," *ArchEph* (1966), pp. 7-14.

[136] As shown by L. Robert, "Inscriptions d'Athènes et de la Grèce centrale," *ArchEph* (1966), p. 14.

[137] *IGRRP* III, 14, with which compare *IGRRP* I, 610; *BCH* (1901), 36 note 184 and E. Ziebarth, *Das griechisches Vereinswesen*, Stuttgart 1896, p. 32 note 1. These references and additional bibliography were collected by L. Robert, "Inscriptions d'Athènes et de la Grèce centrale," *ArchEph* (1966), p. 9.

possessed a "house," the οἶκος Κηρύκων.[138] This "House of the Kerykes" is evidently a building, and as this οἶκος is mentioned closely after an οἰκία it seems that some distinction exists between the two terms. At least two Attic phratries may have possessed "clubhouses," οἰκίαι.[139]

Even more significant is an inscription of the Chian phratry of the Klytidai.[140] In this document again οἶκος and οἰκία are strictly differentiated: it is ordered that an οἶκος be built in the temenos of the Klytidai, and the holy objects be brought from the private houses (ἰδιωτικαὶ οἰκίαι) to the common house (κοινὸς οἶκος).[141]

In one instance a Kleisthenic deme possessed an οἶκος. A building in the deme of Melite was known as the οἶκος Μελιτέων. The evidence for this building has so far gone unnoticed by those scholars concerned with the οἶκος Δεκελειῶν. For the reader's convenience I reproduce the two citations which inform us of the name.

Zenobios II, 27:[142] ἐν τῷ Μελιτέων· ἐλλείπει τὸ οἴκῳ· μέμνηται αὐτῆς Ἀριστοφάνης ἐν Γεωργοῖς καὶ Πλάτων ὁ κωμικός· ἦν δὲ οὗτος ὁ οἶκος μέγας εἰς ὑποδοχὴν μισθούμενος.

At the Meliteans': the word οἴκῳ has fallen out. Aristophanes mentions it in his play "The Farmers" as does Plato the comic poet. This was a big house which was rented out as a hotel.

Hesychios s.v. Μελιτέων οἶκος:[143] ἐν τῷ τῶν Μελιτέων δήμῳ οἶκός τις ἦν παμμεγέθης, εἰς ὃν τραγῳδοὶ <φοιτῶντες> ἐμελέτων.

---

[138] IG II² 1672, line 24. See also SIG² 439 note 26; 587 note 27. F. Maier, Griechischen Mauerbauinschriften, Heidelberg 1959-1961, no. 20, pp. 91-103, may be consulted for further bibliography.

[139] IG II² 1241, lines 18, 32, 41; IG II² 2622, line 2.

[140] SIG³ 987. See also M. Guarducci, "L'istituzione della fratria nella Grecia antica e nelle colonie greche di Italia," parte prima, MAL ser. 6, 6 (1937), no. 18, pp. 63-64.

[141] The significance of the distinction between οἶκος and οἰκία in the documents of the Kerykes and Klytidai is elusive. R. Schöll, "Die kleisthenischen Phratrien," SBAW (1889), part 2, p. 20, for example, argued that οἶκος as opposed to οἰκία in these documents meant "meeting place," and suggested that the οἶκος Δεκελειῶν had a similar meaning.

[142] Compare I. Bekker, Anecdota Graeca, Berlin 1814-1821, I, p. 281, line 25.

[143] Compare the corrupt entry in the Etymologicum Magnum, s.v.

House of the Meliteans: in the deme of Melitai there was a certain huge house, to which the tragedians used to go and rehearse.

It emerges that the οἶκος of the Meliteans was a building situated in the deme of the same name, which was reputedly used for dramatic rehearsals and as an hotel.[144] One scholar has suggested that the οἶκος Μελιτέων was the deme's formal meeting place, but he has been able to adduce no corroborating parallels.[145]

The name of the building, οἶκος Μελιτέων, and the name of the association, οἶκος Δεκελειῶν, are superficially similar, but in the former case the word οἶκος clearly refers to a building, in the latter to a group. If, however, the name of the corporation derives from the clubhouse in which it met, as I have suggested, then the parallel of the οἶκος Μελιτέων becomes much more significant: the οἶκος of the Dekeleians would take its name from a building which, like the οἶκος of the Meliteans, was located in an homonymous deme. As the "house of the Meliteans" belongs to the demesmen, so should the "house of the Dekeleians." It is very likely that both the Μελιτεῖς and Δεκελειεῖς are demesmen.

Since attestations of the οἶκος Μελιτέων do not spell out any connection with the deme of Melitai beyond the purely topographical, I do not choose to press the point. The final analysis of the identity of the οἶκος Δεκελειῶν must rest on the interpretation of its role in the "extraordinary" scrutiny and its relationship to the Demotionidai in this document.

The corporate name οἶκος derives from the building in which the corporation met, and not from any putative familial relationships among its members. The physical "house" of the Dekeleians was in the deme of Dekeleia, and given the isolation of the deme, it may be supposed that the group which used the building was a local body. A variety of groups, including γένη, phratries and demes might meet in, and hence conceivably call themselves, οἶκοι. The οἶκος of the Dekeleians may be any of these. Since, however, the word Δεκελειεῖς is securely attested only as the demotic, and since the deme of Melite is known to have possessed an οἶκος, I am

---

[144] Since the ultimate source of the information is Attic comedy in the persons of Aristophanes (F. 115 Kock) and Plato Comicus (F. 213 Kock), and since there is an evident pun on οἶκος Μελιτέων and ἐμελέτων, the connection between drama and the building should be regarded with some suspicion.

[145] E. Honigmann, *RE* 15, 1 (1931), Melite no. 9, col. 542. For further discussion of the οἶκος Μελιτέων see A. Keramopoulos, "Τὸ Βουλευτήριον τῶν Τεχνιτῶν ἐν Αθήναις," *AD* 11 (1927-1928), pp. 121-122.

strongly disposed to regard the οἶκος Δεκελειῶν as a name for the assembly of demesmen.[146]

Line 36: The oath sworn by the συνήγοροι appointed by the House of the Dekeleians is remarkably similar to the oath sworn by the συνήγοροι appointed by the deme of Myrrhinous:[147] [καὶ] το[ὺ]ς σ[υν]ηγό[ρ]ους συνηγορήσειν τῶι δήμωι τ[ὰ δ]ίκαια καὶ ψ[ηφ]ιεῖσθαι ἃ ἄν μοι δοκεῖ δικαιότατα εἶναι. The συνήγοροι of Myrrhinous are required to swear this oath by Zeus, Apollo and Demeter.

In contrast to the oath of the συνήγοροι of Myrrhine, that of the συνήγοροι of the "House of the Dekeleians" is not guaranteed by Zeus Phratrios or any other god. It is the only oath mentioned in these decrees which omits divine sanctions. If the "House of the Dekeleians" is the phratry or a part of the phratry, this omission is peculiar. If, on the other hand, this group corresponds to the local deme, then the absence of the phratry's gods is not remarkable.

Lines 37-38: The verb φρατρίζω is used only here in the inscription. In the context of this line, commentators have usually translated it as "to join a phratry." So this phrase has been rendered "not to allow anyone who is not qualified to *become a phrater*."[148]

The word φρατρίζεν, however, can have nothing to do with admission to a phratry. The verb εἰσάγω is regularly and consistently used to describe that procedure, both in this inscription and in all testimonia for the Attic phratry.[149] In contrast, the verb φρατρίζω means "to be a member of a phratry."[150] If these lines dealt with admission, φρατρίζεν would have to be replaced with some form of εἰσάγω, for example, ὃκ ἐάσεν ὀδένα μὴ ὄντα

---

[146] Demes normally refer to themselves by either the plural of their demotic or as δημόται. Usually they met in an agora. See *IG* II² 1180, and G.E.M. de Ste. Croix, *The Origins of the Peloponnesian War*, Ithaca 1972, pp. 400-401. No deme decrees of the Meliteans or Dekeleians have been preserved to bear witness to their practices.

[147] *IG* II² 1183, lines 14-16.

[148] Wade-Gery, *Demotionidai*, p. 120, for example, translates this line ambiguously: "not to allow any man who is not a *phrater* to be in the phratry." This translation is not incorrect, but it is misleading, since it implies, at least in contemporary American English, that the issue here may be *admission* to the phratry (to allow someone to *be in* the phratry).

[149] For the use of εἰσάγω see the commentary to lines 18-19: ὃς δ' ἄν δόξηι μὴ ὤν φράτηρ ἐσαχθῆναι: "if it is decided that someone has been introduced though not qualified."

[150] See especially *FGrHist* 342 (Krateros) F. 4, where the verb is used clearly and unambiguously with the meaning "be a member of a phratry." Compare also the *Etymologicum Magnum s.v.* φράτορες; [Dem.] 43, 11-15. The etymology of the word provides some small confirmation of my contention: denominative verbs ending in -ίζω normally connote action, not states of being or becoming: see, *e.g.*, Smyth, *GG*, no. 866.6.

φράτερα ἐσάγεσθαι. Accordingly, this phrase should be translated: "not to allow anyone who is not a *phrater* to continue to be a *phrater*."

Lines 44-45: The demonstrative ταῦτα normally refers to the passage immediately preceding it: that is, to the description of the appeal, or to the entire decree to this point.[151] It seldom refers to a passage following.[152] In this instance the context confirms the rule: the decree continues to make provision for the implementation of the "extraordinary" scrutiny in years to come. Each year the phratriarch is to put the vote to the *phrateres* whether there is anyone in the phratry who needs to be scrutinized, thus perpetuating the proceedings which were described in lines 13-44 and initiated here.

Line 52: For the restoration, compare line 44.

Lines 52-53: Lines 60-61 vouch for the accuracy of the restoration.

Line 55: There is no doubt that the final letter of the word is an A, nor is the number of letters in the word in question. Because of the A the number to be restored cannot be a multiple of one hundred. It is likely, nonetheless, that a round number would be used. Fifty, πεντήκοντα, fills the space exactly, as would eighty, ὀγδοήκοντα, or ninety, ἐνενήκοντα.

Line 59: The text of the decree of Hierokles breaks off after line 57 on the first side. Since no part of the original limits of the bottom of the *stele* survive, there is no way of saying how many lines may have been lost.[153] It is certain that the second side continues the text of the decree of Hierokles, for it commences by referring to the legitimate reasons for which the sacrifice might be made elsewhere than at the altar at Dekeleia. This is surely a reference to the requirement made on face A at lines 52-54 that *phrateres* sacrifice on the altar at Dekeleia. In addition, the *stoichedon* grid at the top of face B has the identical measurements as the grid used for the decree of Hierokles on face A (see Chapter 2, Epigraphical Notes). Since face A ends

---

[151] First noticed by R. Schöll, "Die kleisthenischen Phratrien," *SBAW* (1889), part 2, p. 9 note 1. He was followed by J.H. Lipsius, "Die Phratrie der Demotionidai," *Leipziger Studien* 16 (1894), p. 168. Most other scholars have ignored the importance of the line.

[152] Smyth, *GG*, nos. 1245, 1247; Schwyzer, *GG*, 209 note 3. τάδε is commonly used in Attic inscriptions, as in prose, to refer to the passage following it. There is at least one exception to the rule, *IG* I³ 4, B line 26 (the Hekatompedon inscription). See above, commentary to line 9.

[153] The average proportions of Greek inscribed *stelai* are 1 (thickness) to 4.5 (width) to 9 (height): see S. Dow, "The List of Athenian Archontes," *Hesperia* 3 (1934), pp. 141-144; *idem*, "The Purported Decree of Themistokles, Stele and Inscription," *AJA* 66 (1962), pp. 354-355. The minimum proportions of the present *stele* are 1 (thickness) to 6 (width) to 13.5 (height): in other words, the preserved dimensions of the stone are considerably larger in their proportions than the norm. On these criteria it would appear unlikely that the *stele* was much longer.

with a reference to the collection of a fine from those who have not sacrificed on the altar at Dekeleia, and face B commences with the words, "if one of these things hinders (a *phrater* from sacrificing on the altar at Dekeleia)," it is a safe assumption that a list of those conditions which might prevent someone from coming to Dekeleia has been obliterated from face A.

The order to "sacrifice at the altar at Dekeleia" was prompted by a failure to do so in the past, as the phrase τὸ δὲ λοιπόν in line 52 shows. The reason for the failure to come to Dekeleia was probably the Peloponnesian War. In the last phase of the war, when the Spartans occupied Dekeleia year round, it must have been impossible for the *phrateres* to return to induct new members. The disturbance enabled foreigners to infiltrate the phratry.

The order to sacrifice at the altar at Dekeleia, following as it does on the provisions for the "extraordinary" scrutiny, should be seen as an attempt to rectify the circumstances which originally led to the need to institute the "extraordinary" scrutiny. It is certainly true that during the Peloponnesian War aliens and people descended from only one Athenian parent managed to obtain Athenian citizenship. The problem was so severe that at the end of the war it was necessary to re-enact the citizenship law of Perikles, but with the *proviso* that those born before the archonship of Eukleides were exempted from its requirements.[154] It may reasonably be supposed that the reference to situations which might hinder a *phrater* from sacrificing on the altar at Dekeleia was prompted by the recollection of circumstances which prevailed at the time of the Dekeleian War, and that such problems were outlined in the missing section. So, Sauppe's restoration of the bottom of face A is probably right in essence: εἰ μὴ λοιμός τις ἔσται ἢ πόλεμος.

Line 62: Dorpia was the first day of the festival of the Apatouria (see the commentary to lines 28-29 above), as this phrase in itself shows: in reckoning the days preceding the festival it would be normal to begin the count backward from the first day.

Lines 63-64: The phrase is repeated in lines 122-123. The area where the Dekeleians met in the city surely may be identified with the barbershop "near the Herms" mentioned by Lysias.[155] The area designated as "by the

---

[154] A survey of the vicissitudes of the citizenship law of Perikles from its inception to 403 B.C. is given by C. Patterson, *Perikles' Citizenship Law of 451/0 B.C.*, Salem 1981. See also P.J. Rhodes, *A Commentary on the Aristotelian Athenaion Politeia*, Oxford 1981, pp. 331-332, and the commentary to line 22 above.

[155] Lysias 23 (*Against Pankleon*), 2, quoted above, commentary to line 33. See R. Wycherley, *Literary and Epigraphical Testimonia* (*Athenian Agora* v.3), Princeton 1957, pp. 103-108.

Herms" was discovered between the Stoa of the King and the recently excavated Stoa Poikile at the northwest entrance of the Classical Agora.[156]

SECTION 6: THE DECREE OF NIKODEMOS

Most scholars have held that the decree of Nikodemos was passed by the phratry very soon after the decree of Hierokles, perhaps even at the same meeting.[157] Now, however, it can be shown that the two decrees were not laid out on the stone at the same time: there is a subtle change in the *stoichedon* pattern from the decree of Hierokles to the decree of Nikodemos (see Chapter 2, Description). Thus the two decrees cannot be exactly contemporary. In addition, it does not seem that the same priest was charged with the erection of both decrees (see above, commentary to line 2 and Chapter 2, Epigraphic Notes). This change implies the lapse of some amount of time between the inscription of the two decrees. The decree of Nikodemos cannot, however, be too much later than the decree of Hierokles, for both were cut by the same hand.

Line 68: Nikodemos (*PA* 10869 and 10870) was a wealthy and important member of the deme of Dekeleia, to judge from the grave monuments of his family.[158] His parents were named Phanias (*PA* 14017) and Philoumene (*PA* 14754). Nikodemos married outside of his deme, taking as wife the daughter of a certain Aischines of Phegous (*PA* 370). The pair had three children: two sons, Phanodemos (*PA* 14032) and Anenkletos (*PA* 930), and a daughter named for her maternal grandmother, Philoumene (*PA* 14753). The entire family was buried together at Dekeleia. The five grave monuments are all dated on stylistic grounds to the first third of the fourth century, with the

---

[156] The question of whether or not there existed a "Stoa of the Herms" will require some rethinking and debate in light of the recent excavations in this area: see T.L. Shear, Jr., "The Athenian Agora, Excavation of 1980-1982," *Hesperia* 33 (1984), pp. 1-57.

[157] Wade-Gery, *Demotionidai*, p. 136 note 2: "Had Theodoros set his graver to work to inscribe the first decree only, he would probably have got a larger or smaller stele ... either, that is, he would have got the decree on to one face or spread himself comfortably over both." See also *RIJG* II, no. 29 p. 219, where the decree is interpreted as a direct modification of the decree of Hierokles; *SIG*³ 921 note 35.

[158] For a stemma, see *PA* 14017 and *IG* II² 5983. The most recent discussion of the family is that of F. Willemsen, "Vom Grabbezirk des Nikodemos in Dekeleia," *MDAI(A)* 89 (1974), pp. 173-191, with plates 71-78. The following inscriptions were erected to commemorate members of Nikodemos' family: *IG* II² 5983; *IG* II² 5980 b; *IG* II² 5980 a; *IG* II² 10607; *IG* II² 12865.

exception of the monument to the parents of Nikodemos,[159] which is dated to the end of the fifth century. The identity of the proposer of the second of the Decrees of the Demotionidai with the son of Phanias and Philoumene is assured by the contemporaneity of the documents as well as the coincidence of the deme.

Lines 68-70: The decree of Nikodemos, like the decree of Menexenos (lines 114-116), opens with a formulaic reference[160] to the laws of the phratry which he wishes to modify: those "earlier decrees" which concern the introduction of children. The proposers of both the second and third decrees, Nikodemos and Menexenos, insist frequently that they are dealing with the admission of *children* only (lines 80-81, 105, 109, 115). The proposer of the first decree, Hierokles, makes no reference to children whatsoever. This difference is significant: the decree of Hierokles is entirely concerned with the "extraordinary" scrutiny of those who have already gained admission to the phratry; it has nothing to do with the scrutiny of children, and so makes no reference to them. In contrast, the decrees of Nikodemos and Menexenos are completely concerned with the regular admission of children to the phratry. By emphasizing that their proposals affect only children, Nikodemos and Menexenos make it clear that they are not modifying the procedure of the "extraordinary" scrutiny as described in the decree of Hierokles.

The reference here to "the earlier decrees" gives some indication of the body of law which existed within this phratry by the end of the fifth century B.C. The "decrees" mentioned here probably do not include the proposal of Hierokles, since it does not concern "the introduction of children," but other, even earlier, decrees. That there were phratry decrees other than that of Hierokles may in any event be inferred from the plural: τὰ ψηφίσματα.

The decree of Hierokles, unlike those of Nikodemos and Menexenos, does not begin with a reference to "earlier decrees" which are to be modified. Hierokles omits the rider because his proposal is entirely unparalleled: it has nothing to do with the customary scrutiny of children, but is entirely concerned with an unprecedented "extraordinary" scrutiny.

Line 72: There is no evidence for a procedure called ἀνάκρισις in any other documentation for the phratry. The word is often used as a technical,

---

[159] *IG* II^2 12865.

[160] On the many echoes of official formulae in these decrees, see above, commentary to line 9. These lines approximate the standard formula for a rider, such as one might find in an official state decree: see W. Larfeld, *Handbuch der griechischen Epigraphie* II, Leipzig 1907, p. 825.

legal term, denoting a preliminary inquiry[161] which determined whether or not a case was admissible to court. This general definition is appropriate in the present context: the ἀνάκρισις is mentioned *before* the description of the διαδικασία. Accordingly, the ἀνάκρισις has been interpreted here as a kind of process of selection, preliminary to this phratry's formal procedure for admission.[162]

Line 73: The term θίασος is most commonly used as a general name for religious associations.[163] This inscription provides the only certain evidence that Attic phratries were divided into θίασοι.[164] In all other cases where θίασοι are assumed to be constituent parts of a phratry, this document is the basis for that assumption.[165]

As Andrewes argued, these θίασοι "do not look like old and deeply rooted institutions."[166] It is clear from the list of θίασοι, *IG* II² 2345, that members of γένη, instead of being grouped together, might be divided among several θίασοι.[167] Furthermore, the organization of θίασοι within the phratry seems suspiciously regular and symmetrical: they have no distinctive names, but are differentiated only by the name of a current, prominent member.

All evidence for the division of phratries into θίασοι dates to the first half of the fourth century. Andrewes noted that Nikodemos "contemplates the possibility that a man might not be able to find three witnesses among his own θιασῶται" (lines 76-78), and that this provision implies the collapse of the system.[168] If the θίασοι had been instituted soon before the decree of

---

[161] A.R.W. Harrison, *The Law of Athens* II, Oxford 1971, pp. 94-105, with the bibliography cited at p. 94 note 6.

[162] *RIJG* II, no. 29 pp. 212 and 219. The procedure of the ἀνάκρισις as described here is discussed at length in Chapter 4.

[163] See Harp. and Suda *s.v.* For general discussion see F. Poland, *Geschichte des griechischen Vereinswesens* (*Gekrönte Preisschrift* 38), Leipzig 1909; W.S. Ferguson, "The Attic Orgeones," *HThR* 37 (1944), pp. 61-140.

[164] Athenaios 5, 185c also mentions phratries and θίασοι together. For discussion of θίασοι and phratries, see W.S. Ferguson, "The Attic Orgeones," *HThR* 37 (1944), pp. 64-67, and, above all, Andrewes, *Philochoros*, pp. 9-12.

[165] The only list of θίασοι which can attributed with any confidence to a phratry is *IG* II² 2345, which dates to the middle of the fourth century B.C. Recently M. Golden, "Demosthenes and the Age of Majority in Athens," *Phoenix* 33 (1979), 25-38, has conjectured that *IG* II² 2343, 2346, 2347 and 2348, are also phratry documents.

[166] Andrewes, *Philochoros*, p. 12.

[167] See W.S. Ferguson, "The Salaminioi of Heptaphyle and Sounion," *Hesperia* 7 (1938), p. 28; Andrewes, *Philochoros*, pp. 10, 12.

[168] Andrewes, *Philochoros*, p. 12.

Nikodemos, say in 404/3, they could not have collapsed so quickly. So he concludes that the θίασοι must have been invented some years before the decree of Nikodemos, perhaps before 413, and that their collapse was due to the Spartan occupation of Dekeleia.

The provision concerning smaller θίασοι does not prove that the θίασοι had begun to collapse when Nikodemos proposed his decree. Nikodemos may simply be anticipating the problems that would be caused by the inevitable fluctuations in the size of such groups: such problems may even have existed from the time when the groups were first instituted. It may also be significant that there is no mention of θίασοι in the decree of Hierokles. This silence may conceivably be taken to imply that the groups did not exist at this time.[169] If so, the θίασοι must have been created in the short span separating the two decrees. In any event, the θίασοι must have been devised before the decree of Nikodemos, and probably in the late fifth or early fourth century.

There is little evidence to indicate why these θίασοι were imposed on the phratries. Andrewes' interpretation is probably best. He observed that in *IG* II² 2345 members of the same *genos* are evidently distributed among several θίασοι. He accordingly inferred that one purpose of the institution of θίασοι was to fragment the membership of powerful γένη which existed within phratries: "the institution of θίασοι may be part of a deliberate democratisation of the phratries."[170]

Line 78: Nikodemos does not mention the name of the phratry anywhere in his decree, but he takes special pains to discriminate the various groups mentioned: the phratry and its subordinate parts (lines 81, 85, 89-90, 96, 99, 102 and 104). Whenever he refers to the entire phratry he qualifies them as ἄπαντες. When he contrasts the entire phratry with the θιασῶται he is careful to call them οἱ ἄλλοι φράτερες. Presumably there might have been some confusion if he omitted to provide such qualifications for the *plenum*: if he called them simply οἱ φράτερες the reader might presume that he was speaking only of the "*phrateres* of the candidate,"[171] that is, θιασῶται and not the entire phratry.

---

169 See below, Chapter 5.

170 Andrewes, *Philochoros*, p. 12.

171 For a fuller discussion of circumlocutions used to describe groups within the phratry, see Chapter 5.

SECTION 7: THE DECREE OF MENEXENOS

The two preceding decrees were cut in a *stoichedon* pattern by the same tidy hand in the early part of the fourth century B.C. The decree of Menexenos was inscribed by a later, sloppier hand, and may be dated on orthographical grounds to the middle of the fourth century, probably later than ca. 360: here -ου- is used consistently for the -o- of the previous decrees,[172] a convention which does not become common before ca. 360.[173] This dating of the decree is confirmed by the prosopographic evidence for the third of the phratry's priests, Theodoros (see the commentary to line 2).

Line 114: The orator of this decree (*PA* 9972) does not seem to be known from any other source.[174] The name Menexenos is not particularly common in Attica, with only about a dozen occurrences.[175] Most of the known bearers of the name come from the deme of Kydathenaion.[176]

Line 118: The verb ἀπογράφεσθαι here seems to mean "to register one's intent to undergo the scrutiny." Such a meaning for the word is parallelled only by its use in the context of athletic contests, where it is used to mean "to register one's intent to compete."[177]

Lines 118-119: Curiously this fairly straightforward phrase has attracted a variety of interpretations.[178] Some have held that πρώτωι here is used in the sense of πρότερον, so translating "in the year before the celebration of the *koureion*."[179] Such a use of πρώτωι is indeed rarely attested, but not before the Christian period.[180] Others,[181] swayed by the similar phrase in lines

---

[172] See line 117: τούς; line 118: κούρεον; line 120: τοῦ δήμου.

[173] Threatte, *GAI* I, pp. 241-258.

[174] In spite of Kirchner's assumptions, *PA* 9972.

[175] In addition to the citations in the *PA* see *SEG* 23, no. 87, line 48.

[176] See Davies, *APF* no. 3773.

[177] L. Robert, "Les épigrammes satiriques de Lucillius," in *L'épigramme grècque* (*Fondation Hardt* 14), Geneva 1969, p. 205 note 1; *Bull. ép.* 71, no. 307, with bibliography there cited.

[178] The bibliography is conveniently summarized by J. Labarbe, "L'age corréspondant au sacrifice du κούρειον et les données historiques du sixième discours d'Isée," *BAB* 39 (1953), p. 362 note 3.

[179] M. Guarducci, "L'istituzione della fratria nella Grecia antica e nelle colonie greche di Italia," parte prima, *MAL* ser. 6, 6 (1937), p. 49; R. Schöll, "Die kleisthenischen Phratrien," *SBAW* (1889), part 2, p. 10.

[180] See R. Schöll, "Die kleisthenischen Phratrien," *SBAW* (1889), part 2, p. 10.

[181] Notably *SIG*² 439 note 48 and *RIJG* II, no. 29 pp. 207 and 223.

27-28, have taken it as in some way the equivalent of ὑστερωι. There are no parallels for such a use of πρώτωι. The problem was resolved when it was pointed out that if ἤ was not taken as a comparative conjunction, the problem vanished.[182] So the phrase must be translated "in the first year (sc. of a child's life), or in that year in which the *koureion* is celebrated."

Line 125: Presumably the sanctuary of Leto is somewhere in the vicinity of Dekeleia, though nothing is known of any such cult there. The only evidence for any cult of Leto in Attica comes from a seat in the Theater of Dionysos, which was reserved for the priestess of Leto and Artemis.[183]

The last two letters of the line, Φ and P, are certain. The word to be restored surely derives from the root of φράτηρ, and it must be neuter. A possible restoration might be "phratry register," φρατερικὸν γραμματεῖον.[184] If so restored, it would be the third name employed in as many occurrences for the phratry archives in these decrees (compare above, commentary to lines 22-23), and it would require the assumption that the text of the decree of Menexenos continued for at least several lines more after the break. Since the passage deals with the preliminary registration of prospective phratry members, a mention of the register here would not be inappropriate.

Some other possible restorations might be "phratry sanctuary," φρατρίον,[185] or "phratry decree," φρατερικὸν ψήφισμα. For the latter, however, there are no parallels.

---

[182] J.H. Lipsius, "Die Phratrie der Demotionidai," *Leipziger Studien* 16 (1894), p. 163; *SIG*³ 921 note 46.

[183] *IG* II² 5156.

[184] Compare [Dem.] 44, 41; Isaios 7, 13-17; Isocrates 8, 88.

[185] On this word see C.W. Hedrick, Jr., "The Phratry Shrines of Attica and Athens," *Hesperia*, forthcoming.

CHAPTER FOUR

INTRODUCTION

Each of the three decrees preserved in this inscription deals with some aspect of the scrutiny, διαδικασία, of phratry members. The decrees of Nikodemos and Menexenos are concerned with the "regular" scrutiny. Every year the phratry would gather to induct new members. Applicants were the offspring of phratry members, introduced by their fathers. Before admission was granted, it had to be shown that the applicant was entitled to enter the phratry. Criterion for admission was legitimacy, as defined by the laws of Athens. Before admitting any candidate, the phratry would examine his background to determine whether or not he met this standard.

In the decree of Hierokles a procedure unique to these decrees is described. Evidently a number of individuals had managed to gain admission to this phratry without undergoing the "regular" scrutiny. Since they had not been examined, their credentials were questionable, to say the least. Accordingly, the phratry decided to examine "those who have not yet undergone the scrutiny in accordance with the law of the Demotionidai" (lines 13-14). Any found to have entered the phratry though unqualified were to be expelled, their names expunged from the phratry registers. This "extraordinary" scrutiny thus amounts to a retroactive examination of the members of the phratry. It is in some superficial respects analogous to the διαψήφισις, or revision of the lexiarchic registers of the deme.[1]

PROCEDURE OF THE "EXTRAORDINARY" SCRUTINY

Virtually all those who have studied this inscription agree on the basic outline of the procedures described in the decree of Hierokles. By this interpretation the decree may be divided in two parts. In the first, lines 13-26, provision is made for the scrutiny of *phrateres* "who have not yet been examined": this is the "extraordinary" scrutiny. The second part, lines 26-68,

---

[1] See Chapter 3, commentary to line 13.

makes provision for the future scrutiny of prospective phratry members: this is the "regular" scrutiny.[2]

I propose some modifications to this outline of the decree. On my interpretation the entire decree of Hierokles is directly concerned only with the "extraordinary" scrutiny. Lines 13-26 describe the "extraordinary" scrutiny; lines 26-29 are a digression which state the normal time when a candidate should undergo the "regular" scrutiny; lines 29-52 resume the description of the "extraordinary" scrutiny, which had been interrupted by lines 26-29; lines 52-68 are a second digression, which specifies the normal place where future "regular" scrutinies are to be held.[3] Both of the digressions are patently aimed at specific violations of the existing rules which have made the institution of the "extraordinary" scrutiny necessary.

Scholars have taken lines 26-68 as a description of the "regular" scrutiny because of the occurrence of the phrase τὸ λοιπόν in line 27. It has been assumed that everything following it must be qualified by it. This same phrase, however, recurs in line 52. If τὸ λοιπόν indicates that what follows it should occur in or for the future, it also implies that what has preceded it does not. If everything following τὸ λοιπόν is governed by it, then the second occurrence of the phrase in line 52 is otiose. It therefore is at least reasonable to suppose that at some point between lines 27 and 52 the proposer, Hierokles, has reverted to his original topic of lines 13-26, the "extraordinary" scrutiny. Examination of the passage proves this to be the case.

Lines 45-48 provide that the phratriarch "shall put the vote each year concerning whom (the *phrateres*) ought to scrutinize." The phrase makes no sense in the context of the "regular" scrutiny. In the normal course of phratry admissions, a candidate would undergo the διαδικασία in the year following the sacrifice of the *koureion* (lines 26-29). It would not be necessary to have a vote to decide who should undergo the scrutiny: anyone who had been involved in the sacrifice of the *koureion* in the preceding year would

---

[2] See, e.g. Wilamowitz, *AuA* II, p. 260: "Jede moderne Erklärung ist ohne weiteres hinfällig, die diese Ausnahmemassregel (i.e. lines 12-26) mit den folgenden dauernden Institutionen vermischt." See also the outline provided by Wade-Gery, *Demotionidai*, p. 125.

[3] The interpretation of J.H. Lipsius, "Die Phratrie der Demotionidai," *Leipziger Studien* 16 (1894), pp. 161-171, is in some ways similar to mine. He too held that lines 26-29 were a digression. He thought, however, that the description of the "extraordinary" scrutiny continued only through line 45. In addition, his only argument for linking lines 13-26 and 29-48 was to posit that the verbs describing "rejection" in lines 31 and 38 (ἀποψηφίσωνται) refer to the same procedure as ἀποδικάζω in line 22: Lipsius, *op. cit.*, p. 168. His point is invalid in the case of line 38, which certainly deals with rejection in the appeal. As will be seen, much stronger arguments exist for maintaining that lines 29-52 continue the description of the "extraordinary" scrutiny begun in lines 13-26.

necessarily do so. Furthermore, in the admittedly much later decree of Menexenos it is required that advance notice be given to the *phrateres* of the names of the candidates who will undergo the scrutiny (lines 116-126). It would be impossible for the *phrateres* to "vote each year on whom it was necessary to scrutinize" if they needed notice of the names of those who were to be introduced. Finally, if the phratry had held such a vote, it would imply that some individuals were not required to undergo the scrutiny. It is clear, however, that the phratry intended that everyone be scrutinized. It was precisely the evasion of the scrutiny by certain elements in the phratry which had led to the institution of the "extraordinary" scrutiny.

It is obvious that lines 45-48 cannot describe the procedure of the "regular" scrutiny. They make excellent sense, however, in the context of the "extraordinary" scrutiny. This passage, I suggest, provides for a *continuous revision* of the phratry's registers: henceforth, each year the phratriarch is formally to ask the phratry whether there are any *current* members who ought to undergo the scrutiny. This procedure is crucial to the implementation of the "extraordinary" scrutiny. It is not stated in lines 13-26 how the phratry will determine what members have "not yet undergone the scrutiny" (line 13). Certainly it would be unrealistic to expect that the culprits would themselves volunteer such information. Lines 45-48 provide a procedure to obtain the information: the phratriarch will ask the assembled *phrateres* to denounce those who have evaded the scrutiny.[4]

Another indication that lines 29-52 do not deal with the "regular" scrutiny is the oath which the five συνήγοροι are required to swear: ὁκ ἐάσεν ὁδένα μὴ ὄντα φράτερα φρατρίζεν (lines 36-38). The phrase means "not to allow anyone who is not qualified to continue to be a member of the phratry."[5] It must be interpreted as a provision for the "extraordinary" scrutiny, which examines people who are already members of the phratry. It makes no sense in the context of the "regular" scrutiny, which deals with applicants to the phratry.

The absence of the introducer from the appeal described in lines 29-52 provides further evidence that this section describes the "extraordinary" scrutiny. In line 31 those who make the appeal are also the object of the verb ἀποψηφίζομαι: ἐὰν δέ τις βόληται ἐφεῖναι ἐς Δημοτιωνίδας ὧν ἄν

---

[4] It should be emphasized here that the phratry is not revising their entire list of members, as the demes did in the διαψήφισις. They are examining only those members who are said *not yet* to have undergone the scrutiny. See Chapter 3, commentary to line 13.

[5] The meaning of this phrase and of φρατρίζειν has been discussed above, Chapter 3, commentary to lines 36-38.

ἀποψηφίσωνται, ἐξεῖναι αὐτῶι, "Anyone whom they reject may appeal to the Demotionidai, if he wishes." The same construction occurs in lines 38-39, when reference is made to "whomever of the appellants whom they reject," ὅτο δ' ἂν τῶν ἐφέντων ἀποψηφίσωνται. In both of these instances, the object of the verb ἀποψηφίζομαι and the subject of the verb ἐφίημι is grammatically the same person. The identity of the person is not specified. In all previous interpretations of the document it has been assumed that this person must be the εἰσάγων, or sponsor.[6]

In the "regular" scrutiny it is clearly the sponsor who makes the appeal. For example, in lines 94-96 Nikodemos allows that "if the θιασῶται reject (him) and the sponsor appeals...," ἐὰν δὲ ἀποψηφίσωνται οἱ θιασῶται, ὁ δὲ εἰσάγων ἐφῆι. Furthermore, in the "regular" scrutiny the sponsor is never the object of the verb ἀποψηφίζομαι; only the candidate can be rejected, because it is only his membership in the phratry which is at issue, not that of his sponsor.[7] The procedure of a negative vote is not discussed in the decree of Menexenos. In the proposal of Nikodemos, however, the term ἀποψηφίζομαι is used five times (lines 90, 95, 98, 101 and 103). The object of the verb is never expressly stated; nevertheless it is always clear in context that a vote of rejection is directed at the candidate.[8]

In lines 31 and 38, then, the person who makes the appeal is identical with the person who is rejected. The introducer cannot be rejected, but only the candidate. So here evidently is a case where the candidate himself makes the appeal, in direct conflict with what is known of the admission procedures in other phratries, and with the provisions made for the regular scrutiny in the decree of Nikodemos. The description of the appeal in these lines, then, is evidently not a part of the "regular" scrutiny, as has commonly been supposed.

The roles of the introducer and candidate in the "extraordinary" scrutiny have never been thoroughly examined. As we have just seen, the introducer evidently had no function in the appeal to the Demotionidai. The fact that the candidate himself undertook this appeal or that he should have had any active role whatsoever is very odd. There are no parallels for such participation by

---

[6] For example, Wade-Gery, *Demotionidai*, p. 120, translates line 30: "If anyone wishes to appeal to the Demotionidai after an adverse vote..."; and at line 38: "any appellant who gets an adverse vote..." He goes on to discuss the passage as though it is the εἰσάγων who appeals and the candidate who is rejected (p. 125): "An introducer whose candidate is rejected..."

[7] See generally the discussion of the verb εἰσάγω above, Chapter 3, commentary to lines 18-19 and note 83.

[8] See, for example, lines 95-103.

the candidate. In the context of phratry admissions, in fact, there is not even a distinct word for candidate: the idea is brought across by a passive form of the verb εἰσάγω.

In normal circumstances the candidate would be a minor, and so could have no active role in his admission to the phratry.[9] The decrees of Nikodemos and Menexenos both deal explicitly with the introduction of children, ἡ εἰσαγωγὴ τῶν παίδων (lines 70 and 115). In both the candidate clearly has no active part in the proceedings. Nikodemos, for example, proposes that when the θιασῶται hold their scrutiny of someone who is being introduced, τὸ εἰσαγομένο (line 82), they will vote secretly. Then if the θιασῶται reject the child, it is the one introducing him, ὁ εἰσάγων, who will appeal to the assembled *phrateres*. In lines 108-113 the witnesses are to swear at the introduction, εἰσαγωγή, that "the one whom he introduces," ὃν εἰσάγει, "is his legitimate child." Menexenos wants the *phrateres* to know in advance "those about to be introduced," τοὺς μέλλοντας εἰσάγεσθαι (line 117).

The verb εἰσάγω is used much less frequently in the decree of Hierokles; it is also used exclusively in the aorist tense. In the entire description of the "extraordinary" scrutiny the verb εἰσάγω appears only twice: in line 19 the aorist passive infinitive occurs, and in line 22 the aorist active participle.

The use of the aorist tense of εἰσάγω in lines 13-26 has, for the most part, been ignored by commentators.[10] These aorists, I suggest, should be interpreted temporally, as referring to a relatively past event.[11] On my interpretation, then, the references to "introduction" in lines 19 and 22 refer to the *original* introduction of the member into the phratry, not to any role that an introducer is to play in the (relatively) present "extraordinary" scrutiny. This explanation would account for both the absence of the verb εἰσάγω from the description of the "extraordinary" scrutiny and for the role of the candidate in the appeal to the Demotionidai: the candidates to whom the decree of Hierokles alludes are evidently adults, individuals who have already been "introduced" into the phratry (though they have not yet

---

[9] Note that under Athenian law, a person who was not a registered adult citizen could not initiate legal proceedings: see P.J. Rhodes, *A Commentary on the Aristotelian Athenaion Politeia*, Oxford 1981, p. 501.

[10] To the best of my knowledge, the only scholar to discuss these aorists is W.E. Thompson, "An Interpretation of the 'Demotionid' Decrees," *SO* 62 (1968), p. 56: "The sponsor of such a candidate (i.e. at the "regular" scrutiny) is called ὁ ἐσάγων, while the sponsor at the special scrutiny is called ὁ ἐσαγάγων."

[11] All of the aorists of the decree of Hierokles should be taken temporally. Compare Chapter 3, commentary to line 22 and note 83.

undergone the διαδικασία: line 13). They are thus expected to take an active part in the proceedings of the "extraordinary" scrutiny. The introducer accordingly has no role, save to pay a fine if it emerges that he *originally* introduced someone who is not qualified into the phratry.

It should now be clear that lines 13-26 and 29-52 both describe the "extraordinary" scrutiny; lines 26-29 are a digression. Lines 29-52, then, continue the description of the "extraordinary" scrutiny, which had been interrupted at line 26. Lines 29-32 allow "anyone whom (they) reject to appeal to the Demotionidai, if he wishes," ἐὰν δέ τις βόληται ἐφεῖναι ἐς Δημοτιωνίδας ὧν ἂν ἀποψηφίσωνται, ἐξεῖναι αὐτῶι. These lines describe the procedure of appeal, ἔφεσις, from a negative judgement. The preceding lines should give an account of some rejection. There is nothing of the sort in lines 26-29, which deal with the appropriate time for the "regular" scrutiny: "from now on the scrutiny will take place in the year following the sacrifice of the *koureion* at the feast of the Apatouria on the day called *Koureotis*. The *phrateres* shall take their ballots from the altar." τὴν δὲ διαδικασίαν τὸ λοιπὸν ἔναι τῶι ὑστέρωι ἔτει ἢ ὧι ἂν τὸ κόρεον θύσηι, τῆι Κορεώτιδι Ἀπατορίων· φέρεν δὲ τὴν ψῆφον ἀπὸ τὸ βωμῶ. The passage is neutral: it does not refer to the rejection of a candidate.[12] However, lines 18-26 do describe a negative vote and the penalties imposed as a result. This section in my opinion describes the negative vote which precedes the appeal of lines 29-32.

Granted that lines 13-26 and 29-52 comprise a continuous description of the "extraordinary" scrutiny, it remains to explain the two sections which do not, i.e. lines 26-29 and 52-64. Both passages are, in my estimation, digressions which relate to the reasons for the implementation of, the "extraordinary" scrutiny.

Lines 26-29 are inserted to provide that the διαδικασία will be administered at the appropriate time in the future, that is, one year after the sacrifice of the *koureion*. It was precisely this dereliction which had prompted the "extraordinary" scrutiny: certain individuals had not undergone the scrutiny at the proper time (i.e. not at all: line 13), so creating a group within

---

[12] Virtually all scholars have supposed that φέρεν τὴν ψῆφον in line 29 is the equivalent of ἀποψηφίζομαι. See, *e.g.*, Wade-Gery, *Demotionidai*, p. 127; Wilamowitz, *AuA*, II, p. 260; compare also the introduction to Chapter 5. This interpretation seems to me inaccurate and tendentious. The phrase φέρεν τὴν ψῆφον ἀπὸ τὸ βωμῶ in these decrees commonly describes a general rule, not a verdict (see, *e.g.*, lines 82-84). The custom of "taking the ballot from the altar" was thought to have the effect of sanctifying the vote (see Chapter 3, commentary to lines 17-18). The phrase in line 29 might almost be translated: "let the *phrateres* vote honestly in the sight of the gods."

the phratry whose status needed to be verified. These lines are intended to prevent the problem from recurring in the future.

Lines 52-64 are appended to insure that the sacrifices of the *meion* and *koureion* take place at Dekeleia on the altar of the phratry. There is nothing in the preceding provisions for the "extraordinary" scrutiny to imply that people had been sacrificing the *meion* and *koureion* elsewhere, but the ominous remark within the digression about "(circumstances) which might prevent people from sacrificing at Dekeleia" (line 59) certainly suggests some such problem. The reference to "hindrances" was doubtless inspired by the recent hardships of the Spartan occupation of Dekeleia. From 413 to 404 it had been impossible for the phratry to return to its ancestral shrine. The digression implies that this traumatic isolation[13] somehow contributed to the breakdown of the phratry's admission procedures. It is not clear precisely what relationship was thought to exist between phratry shrine and διαδικασία. Perhaps the phratry felt it could exercise greater control over members and candidates, or that the scrutiny was conducted with more propriety and greater severity when the meeting was held at Dekeleia.

In closing I provide an outline of the procedure of the "extraordinary" scrutiny as I construct it. Digressions concerning the "regular" scrutiny are enclosed in square brackets:

Lines 13-18: Anyone who has not yet done so is to undergo the scrutiny immediately.

Lines 18-26: If it is discovered at the "extraordinary" scrutiny that the original introduction of a *phrater* was illegal, his name shall be expunged from the phratry registers; the person who originally introduced him without submitting him to the scrutiny is to pay a fine of one hundred drachmai.

[*Lines 26-29*: In the future everyone shall undergo the "regular" scrutiny in the year following the sacrifice of the *koureion*.]

Lines 29-32: If a *candidate* wishes, he may appeal the adverse decision (see lines 18-26) to the Demotionidai.

Lines 32-37: The House of the Dekeleians will appoint five συνήγοροι to serve with the Demotionidai in judging the appeals.

---

[13] See Thucydides 2, 16, with the discussion in C.W. Hedrick, Jr., "The Phratry Shrines of Attica and Athens," *Hesperia*, forthcoming.

Lines 38-44: Any *candidate* rejected in the appeal is to pay a fine of one thousand drachmai.

Line 45: The procedure of the "extraordinary" scrutiny is to be in effect beginning with the archonship of Phormion.

Lines 45-52: The phratriarch is charged to implement the "extraordinary" scrutiny in succeeding years; each year he shall put the vote to the phratry whether there is anyone in the phratry who needs to be scrutinized. If the phratriarch does not put the vote, he shall be subject to a fine of five hundred drachmai.

[*Lines 52-64*: It is required that the "regular" sacrifices of the *meion* and *koureion* take place on the phratry altar at Dekeleia in the future. If (for any of several reasons) it is impossible to do so, the priest shall post the name of the place where the sacrifice is to be offered.]

THE "REGULAR" SCRUTINY

In contrast with the decree of Hierokles, the decrees of Nikodemos and Menexenos are both explicitly concerned with the procedure of the "regular" scrutiny, that is, with the scrutiny of children. In formulaic preambles both announce that they will modify "previous decrees concerning the introduction of children," τὰ μὲν ἄλλα κατὰ τὰ πρότερα ψηφίσματα ἃ κῆται περὶ τῆς εἰσαγωγῆς τῶν παίδων (lines 68-70, 114-116).[14] This concern is confirmed by the frequent reference to children, particularly in the decree of Nikodemos (lines 70, 80, 105, 110).

The decree of Menexenos is considerably later and shorter than the first two decrees. It makes a relatively minor contribution to the regulations governing the "regular" scrutiny and so has attracted little attention from commentators. Menexenos provides that the names of "those about to be introduced" be posted, along with the patronymic and demotic of their father and maternal grandfather. The list is to be posted in advance of the εἰσαγωγή, once in the candidate's first year and again in the year when the sacrifice of the *koureion* is to be held (lines 118-120). Presumably children underwent the εἰσαγωγή on these two occasions.

---

14 The reference in the decree of Menexenos to τὰ πρότερα ψηφίσματα doubtless includes the decree of Nikodemos, even though Menexenos nowhere specifically emends it.

The decree of Nikodemos may be used to compose a summary outline of the "regular" scrutiny:

Lines 68-71: Nikodemos reaffirms the validity of the previous decrees dealing with the introduction and scrutiny of children, with the exception of the modifications which he is about to propose.

Lines 71-78: The three witnesses at the ἀνάκρισις must be furnished from among the θιασῶται of the candidate, unless there are not enough θιασῶται to fill the number. Failing θιασῶται, the witnesses are to be provided from among the other *phrateres*.

Lines 78-106: When the διαδικασία takes place, the phratriarch shall not permit the entire phratry to vote until the candidate's θιασῶται have voted. If the θιασῶται admit the candidate, the entire phratry must still approve him. If the θιασῶται reject the candidate, the sponsor has the option of appealing the decision to the entire phratry.

Lines 106-108: The priest is to add the decree of Nikodemos to the marble *stele*.

Lines 108-113: The text of the oath which the witnesses must swear at "the introduction of children" is published.

The various elements of the procedure are clearly marked in the decree. Throughout Nikodemos is careful to deal with each subject distinctly. He opens by announcing the topics of his decree: the εἰσαγωγή and διαδικασία (lines 70-71). When he turns to the ἀνάκρισις, he begins with the words τὸς δὲ μάρτυρας τρῆς, ὃς εἴρηται ἐπὶ τῆι ἀνακρίσει παρέχεσθαι (lines 71-72). When the topic changes to the διαδικασία he marks the transition by saying ὅταν δε ἦι ἡ διαδικασία (lines 78-79). When he turns from the διαδικασία to the witnesses and their oath, he labels the oath: ὅρκος μαρτύρων ἐπὶ τῆι εἰσαγωγεῖ τῶν παίδων (lines 108-109).

The relationship of Nikodemos' decree to the existing laws and regulations of the phratry, and particularly to the decree of Hierokles, is controversial. The decree begins with a reference to the regulations which it modifies: τὰ πρότερα ψηφίσματα ἃ κεται περὶ τῆς εἰσαγωγῆς τῶν παίδων καὶ τῆς διαδικασίας (lines 69-71).

Some scholars have argued that this phrase refers to all former decrees of the phratry, *including* the decree of Hierokles.[15] Wade-Gery even suggested that the decree of Nikodemos was moved at the same meeting of the phratry as the decree of Hierokles, and was a direct and specific response to it.[16] Nikodemos, however, specifies the decrees which he wishes to modify: those which pertain to the introduction of children and the scrutiny. As I have argued, the decree of Hierokles has nothing to do with the introduction of *children*, and seems concerned with the procedure of the διαδικασία only insofar as people have not undergone it. If the decree of Hierokles modified the regulations of the "regular" scrutiny at all (and I do not think this is likely), it can only have done so in the two parenthetical sections, lines 26-29 and 52-68. The wording of the decree of Nikodemos does not suggest that it modifies the decree of Hierokles. To the contrary, the frequent reference to children explicitly excludes the possibility of any allusion to the "extraordinary" scrutiny.

The preamble of the decree of Nikodemos refers to "earlier *decrees.*" The use of the plural here proves that there were other, earlier decrees than that of Hierokles. This inference is confirmed by the decree of Hierokles itself, which refers to a νόμος Δημοτιωνιδῶν: "if someone has not been scrutinized according to the law of the Demotionidai, let the *phrateres* do so immediately" (line 14). The existence of a νόμος implies a body of rules and regulations governing the procedure of the scrutiny. The phrase τὰ πρότερα ψηφίσματα, I suggest, corresponds to the νόμος Δημοτιωνιδῶν.

At the beginning of his decree, Nikodemos announces that he will modify two particular procedures: the εἰσαγωγή and the διαδικασία. He proceeds to describe the διαδικασία in lines 78-106 and, in lines 108-113, he quotes the oath of the witnesses at the εἰσαγωγή. In lines 71-78, however, he describes a third procedure: the ἀνάκρισις.

The ἀνάκρισις is apparently a kind of "preliminary hearing" (see Chapter 3, commentary to line 72). Nikodemos is concerned only with the role of witnesses in this procedure: they are preferably to come from the θίασος of the candidate; they are to answer questions under oath, and to swear by Zeus Phratrios; as they swear they are to cling to the altar.

---

[15] See R. Schöll, "Die kleisthenischen Phratrien," *SBAW* (1889), part 2, p. 5 note 2; J.H. Lipsius, "Die Phratrie der Demotionidai," *Leipziger Studien* 16 (1894), p. 162 note 2; *RIJG* II, no. 29 p. 212.

[16] *Demotionidai*, p. 125. His suggestion is certainly incorrect: see Chapter 3, commentary to line 2.

The word εἰσαγωγή means "introduction." It is mentioned in the decree only in an appendix,[17] which cites "the oath of the witnesses at the εἰσαγωγή of children." These witnesses are to swear that the child introduced is legitimate. The oath is sworn in the name of Zeus Phratrios.

The ἀνάκρισις is not mentioned in the preamble, though it is described in the decree; the εἰσαγωγή, which is mentioned in the preamble, is not described in the decree. The role of the witnesses at the ἀνάκρισις is emphasized; the oath of witnesses at the εἰσαγωγή is quoted. It appears possible, even likely, that ἀνάκρισις and εἰσαγωγή are alternative names for the identical procedure.

The διαδικασία consists of two parts: a preliminary, secret ballot by the θιασῶται of the candidate; then, if they approve the candidate, a final ballot by the entire phratry. If the candidate was rejected in the final ballot the θιασῶται who admitted him were to pay a fine, "except for those of the *thiasotai* who appear to have spoken against the admission, or to have opposed it at the διαδικασία": πλὴν ὅσοι ἂν τῶν θιασωτῶν κατήγοροι ἢ ἐναντιόμενοι φαίνωνται ἐν τῆι διαδικασίαι (lines 92-94). If the θιασῶται rejected a candidate, the introducer had the option of appealing the decision to the entire phratry. If he did not do so, the rejection of the θιασῶται was final. If the introducer did appeal and the entire phratry rejected the candidate, then he, the introducer, paid a fine. When the entire phratry voted, the θιασῶται of the candidate were not allowed to take part.

Wade-Gery maintained that the preliminary ballot of the θιασῶται was not technically a part of the διαδικασία: the preliminary vote is secret (lines 81-82), and so it should be impossible for any of the θιασῶται to make their opposition known; yet, in lines 92-94 penalties are prescribed for those θιασῶται who do not openly oppose an unqualified candidate at the διαδικασία. Consequently he concluded that only the judgement of the entire phratry was properly called the διαδικασία. The procedure of the preliminary vote of the θιασῶται, he argued, was a modification to the phratry's νόμος, introduced by Nikodemos.[18]

In my opinion, Wade-Gery's interpretation of the preliminary vote is unwarranted. It is most natural to construe line 79, ὅταν δὲ ἦι ἡ διαδικασία, as introducing a description of the διαδικασία. The wording of this

---

[17] The oath is clearly an appendix, because it is inscribed after the provisions for the publication of the decree.

[18] Wade-Gery, *Demotionidai*, p. 127.

description implies that the preliminary vote was part of the διαδικασία. It does not suggest that the preliminary vote was an innovation of Nikodemos.

Wade-Gery's main argument is indisputable: the θιασῶται cannot publicly oppose a candidate in a secret ballot, and therefore this public opposition must occur at the judgement before the entire phratry. His conclusion, however, that only the vote of the entire phratry is called the διαδικασία, does not necessarily follow from this argument. Certainly it is clear that the word διαδικασία in line 94 cannot refer *exclusively* to the preliminary, secret ballot. If, however, both preliminary and final votes are subsumed under the general name διαδικασία, as line 79 implies, then line 94 poses no problem.

There is nothing in lines 78-106 which suggests that the preliminary scrutiny is instituted for the first time in the decree of Nikodemos. Rather, it appears that the preliminary scrutiny had been by-passed in certain cases, and that the phratriarch is being ordered to guard against these abuses. In the introductory sentence (lines 78-84) the emphasis is surely on the main clause: "let the phratriarch not offer the vote to the entire phratry before the thiasotai hold a secret ballot." If Nikodemos were instituting the preliminary scrutiny for the first time, the order of the clauses would have been reversed: "Let the θιασῶται hold a secret ballot before the phratriarch offers the vote to the entire phratry."

THE "REGULAR" AND "EXTRAORDINARY" SCRUTINIES

Most scholars have stressed the singularity of the procedure described in the decree of Hierokles.[19] It is universally agreed that the διαδικασία as described in the decree of Hierokles should not be explained in terms of the procedure described in the decree of Nikodemos. I suggest that the two procedures are identical.

In the decree of Hierokles the "extraordinary" retroactive διαδικασία is described. This procedure is divided into two parts: the *phrateres* are to scrutinize those who have not yet undergone the διαδικασία; if they reject the candidate, he may appeal to the Demotionidai.

In the decree of Nikodemos the "regular" διαδικασία of *prospective* members is described. This procedure involves two votes: the θιασῶται of the candidate vote first (lines 84-86); if they admit him, their vote must be

---

[19]   For a clear assertion of this singularity, see Wilamowitz, *AuA*, II, p. 260.

ratified by the entire phratry; if they reject him, the introducer has the option of appealing to the entire phratry; if the candidate chooses not to appeal, then the rejection by the θιασῶται is final.

In outline the "extraordinary" scrutiny and the "regular" scrutiny are obviously very similar. In both the procedure consists first of a scrutiny before one body.[20] If that group rejects the candidate, appeal is allowed from it to another body.[21] It should be noted, however, that Hierokles does not describe the consequences of a decision of the first group in as much detail as Nikodemos. He does not specify that a rejection by οἱ φράτερες is final if no appeal is made (though this is logically the case). He does not state that acceptance by οἱ φράτερες must be validated by the Demotionidai.

As the two scrutinies are similar in practice, they are in name identical. The word διαδικασία is used to describe both. If these two procedures were distinct, they would have distinguishable names.

Hierokles himself implies that the "extraordinary" scrutiny will not differ procedurally from the "regular" scrutiny. He explicitly states the purpose of the "extraordinary" scrutiny in line 13: ὁπόσοι μήπω διεδικάσθησαν κατὰ τὸν νόμον τὸν Δημοτιωνιδῶν, διαδικάσαι περὶ αὐτῶν τὸς φράτερας. Hierokles intends that "the *phrateres* scrutinize those who have not yet undergone the scrutiny." Since the purpose of the "extraordinary" scrutiny is to correct earlier irregularities in the admissions procedure of the phratry, it would be shocking if it were itself irregular. Surely the scrutiny which has been avoided (διεδικάσθησαν) and that to come (διαδικάσαι) are identical.

There is, then, no obvious reason to distinguish the procedure of the "extraordinary" scrutiny from that of the "regular" scrutiny. To the contrary, so far as can be determined from the decrees of Hierokles and Nikodemos, the two are virtually identical. The "extraordinary" scrutiny is evidently "extraordinary" only insofar as it examines current members of the phratry rather than candidates.

---

[20] In the decree of Hierokles this body is described as οἱ φράτερες; in that of Nikodemos as οἱ θιασῶται.

[21] In the decree of Hierokles to the Δημοτιωνίδαι; in that of Nikodemos to οἱ ἅπαντες φράτερες.

CHAPTER FIVE

THE DEMOTIONIDAI AND THE HOUSE OF THE DEKELEIANS

INTRODUCTION

Arguably the most important problem in the interpretation of these decrees is the identification of the two groups mentioned: the Demotionidai and the House of the Dekeleians. Indisputably the evaluation of these two groups and their relationship has provoked more scholarly controversy than any other question raised by the document.

The essentials of the problem were first articulated by E. Szanto in 1885.[1] Up to that time scholars had assumed without argument that the name of the phratry was Demotionidai.[2] Szanto pointed out that appeal (ἔφεσις) was allowed from a decision of the phratry (the assumed subject of φέρεν in line 29 and ἀποψηφίσωνται in line 31) to the Demotionidai (line 30). If these two groups were identical, he argued, the word ἔφεσις was improperly used: it would have been unparalleled (and pointless) for a candidate to appeal to the same group which has rejected him. Szanto therefore concluded that Demotionidai was not the name of the phratry, but of some privileged group within the phratry, probably a *genos*. He identified the House of the Dekeleians as the phratry, because of its evident authority and concern in the procedure of the appeal to the Demotionidai.[3]

Virtually none of Szanto's contemporaries accepted his identification of the Demotionidai and House of the Dekeleians. Nevertheless, his arguments were compelling; their strength may be gauged by the variety and number of immediate attacks which they provoked.[4] No one could dispute Szanto's

---

[1] E. Szanto, "Zur attischen Phratrien- und Geschlechterverfassung," *RhM* 40 (1885), pp. 506-520. It should be noted that when Szanto wrote his essay he did not have access to the entire text: face B of the inscription had not yet been deciphered.

[2] See S. Koumanoudes, "Ψήφισμα Φρατερικόν," *ArchEph* (1883), cols. 69-76; U. Köhler, commentary to *IG* II, 2, addenda 841 b.

[3] E. Szanto, "Zur attischen Phratrien- und Geschlechterverfassung," *RhM* 40 (1885), pp. 508, 511.

[4] For a summary review of the scholarship to 1905 see R. Schöll, *RE* 5 (1905), Demotionidai, cols. 194-202. The only scholar to follow Szanto's lead in print was W.R. Paton, "Comment on Tarbell's 'Study of an Attic Phratry,' " *AJA* 6 (1890), pp. 314-318; *idem*, "The Decelean Inscription and Attic Phratries," *CR* 5 (1891), pp. 221-223.

central point: a decision cannot be appealed to the same group which has rendered it. Everyone, however, agreed that the Demotionidai had to be the phratry. The appeal was made to the Demotionidai, therefore the initial rejection must have been rendered by some group other than the phratry. It was generally agreed that this initial rejection was described by the phrase φέρεν δὲ τὴν ψῆφον ἀπὸ τὸ βωμὸ (line 29). The subject of this phrase is unexpressed.

After Szanto's article, most scholars focused on the identity of the group which had rendered the initial judgement. C. Schäffer, for example, argued that the "pre-Kleisthenic phratry of the Demotionidai" had, in classical times, fragmented into smaller phratries. One of these smaller phratries, he suggested, rendered the preliminary judgement, and the entire phratry of the Demotionidai judged the appeal.[5] H. Sauppe, comparing the procedure described in the decree of Nikodemos, suggested that the preliminary judgement was rendered by θιασῶται, and that appeal was made from them to the entire phratry.[6] Others argued that the appeal was made to the same body which had voted the preliminary rejection, that is, from the phratry to the phratry. They justified their position by contending that the term ἔφεσις was used imprecisely,[7] or by claiming that the judicial character of the phratry changed with the character of the case it was judging: that is, insofar as the phratry judged the appeal, it was, *ipso facto*, not the same body which had passed the preliminary rejection.[8] Wilamowitz offered the idea that the preliminary decision was rendered by the "House of the Dekeleians," and that appeal was allowed from its decision to the Demotionidai, that is, to the phratry.[9]

---

[5] C. Schäffer, *Altes und Neues über die attischen Phratrie*, Naumberg 1888, p. 30.

[6] H. Sauppe, "Commentatio de phratriis altera," *Index scholarum in Academia Georgia Augusta*, 1890, p. 6. See lines 94 and 100 of the decree of Nikodemos, where preliminary judgement is rendered by the θιασῶται and appeal is made "to the whole." See also G. Gilbert, "Der Beschluss der Phratrie der Demotionidai," *JbPh* 135 (1887), pp. 23-28 and *idem*, *Greek Constitutional Antiquities* II (English translation of the 1893 edition of his *Griechischen Staatsalterthümer*), London 1895, p. 261 note 1.

[7] F.B. Tarbell, "The Decrees of the Demotionidai, a Study of the Attic Phratry," *AJA* 5 (1889) pp. 135-153; *idem*, "Mr. Tarbell's Reply to Mr. Paton's Comment," *AJA* 6 (1890), pp. 318-320.

[8] R. Schöll, "Die kleisthenischen Phratrien," *SBAW* (1889), part 2, pp. 8-9; J.H. Lipsius, "Die Phratrie der Demotionidai," *Leipziger Studien* 16 (1894), p. 168.

[9] Wilamowitz, *AuA* II, p. 261. A similar idea was proposed by J. Pantazides, "'Επιγραφὴ ἐκ Δεκελείας," *ArchEph* (1888), cols. 15-18.

For more than thirty years after the studies of Wilamowitz and Lipsius there were no new attempts to deal with the procedure of the appeal and the identities of the two groups. Scholars were aware of the difficulties in the interpretation of the passage. All agreed, however, that Demotionidai was the name of the phratry.[10] Then in 1931 H.T. Wade-Gery published what is surely the most influential study of the problem.[11] In this article he revived with some modifications the views of Szanto and argued persuasively against the interpretation of Wilamowitz. In his opinion, the preliminary decision could only have been rendered by the phratry. He concluded that House of the Dekeleians was the name of the phratry and Demotionidai was the name of a *genos* within the phratry. Since the publication of this article, there have been few discussions devoted to the fundamental problems raised by "the appeal to the Demotionidai." Most scholars instead have built upon the views of either Wade-Gery or Wilamowitz.[12] Accordingly, in setting forth my own views I shall address most of my remarks to these two, most influential, essays.

---

[10] In most commentaries of the period this identification is assumed. See, for example, *RIJG* II, no. 29; *SIG*[3] 921; Busolt-Swoboda 1920-1926, p. 962 note 3.

[11] Wade-Gery, *Demotionidai.*

[12] See for example the famous essay by Andrewes, *Philochoros*, pp. 4-5. After reviewing exclusively the arguments of Wilamowitz and Wade-Gery, he comes down decisively on the side of the latter: "I take it, then, that Demotionidai were a genos with a privileged position inside the phratry Dekeleies." I believe that the consensus of scholarly opinion currently favors Wade-Gery's views: see M. Guarducci, "L'istituzione della fratria nella Grecia antica e nelle colonie greche di Italia," parte prima, *MAL* ser. 6, 6 (1937), p. 43; W. Thompson, "An Interpretation of the 'Demotionid' Decrees," *SO* 62 (1968), pp. 51-68. Relatively few scholars have committed themselves to the interpretation of Wilamowitz: see for example M. Just, *Die Ephesis in der Geschichte des attischen Prozesses-- ein Versuch zur Deutung der Rechtsnatur der Ephesis* (Thesis Würzburg), Würzburg 1965, pp. 280-322; D. Roussel, *Tribu et cité (Annales littéraires de l'Université de Besançon,* v. 193), Paris 1976, p. 151 note 54. Rarely has anyone opted for one of the other, older interpretations: S.C. Humphreys, *Anthropology and the Greeks,* London 1978, p. 26, for example, follows Tarbell and Schöll (cited above, notes 7 and 8). See further the relatively recent discussions of the problem in M.P. Nilsson, *Cults, Myths, Oracles and Politics in Ancient Greece,* 1951 (reprint New York 1972), pp. 150-170; F. Bourriot, *Récherches sur la nature du génos: étude d'histoire sociale Atheniènne--périodes archaïque et classique,* Lille 1976, pp. 639-648. S.D. Lambert develops an interpretation of the decrees which is similar, in certain respects, to that of Schäffer (cited above, note 5) in his recent Oxford dissertation, *The Ionian Phyle and Phratry in Archaic and Classical Athens* (Thesis, Oxford), Ann Arbor 1986; for the main outline of the decrees, however, he adheres to the interpretation of Wade-Gery. Lambert also provides a detailed critique of the interpretation which I offer here. Lambert informs me that he intends to publish a version of his dissertation presently. I have been unable to examine in detail L.M. Gluskina, "Phratry and Clan in Fourth Century Athens," *VDI* 165 (1983), pp. 39-52 (Russian with English summary) or Sadao Ito, "An Interpretation of the so-called Demotionid Inscription," *The Journal of History* (Kyoto) 71 (1988), pp. 677-713 (Japanese with English summary).

THIASOS, PHRATERES AND DEMOTIONIDAI

Virtually all of these interpretations of the Demotionidai and House of the Dekeleians have been based on a misunderstanding of the decree of Hierokles and of the "extraordinary" scrutiny. Since the discovery of the inscription, scholars have assumed that Hierokles' description of the "extraordinary" scrutiny ends at line 18, and that lines 19-67 concern the "regular" scrutiny.[13] As I have argued (above, Chapter 4), however, the entire decree of Hierokles is concerned with the "extraordinary" scrutiny. The procedure of this "extraordinary" scrutiny, as I revise it, is closely paralleled by the procedure of the "regular" scrutiny. This revision of the outline of the "extraordinary" scrutiny and its now apparent parallel with the procedure of the "regular" scrutiny make possible a reassessment of the identities of the Demotionidai and of the House of the Dekeleians.

The procedures of the "regular" and "extraordinary" scrutinies are obviously very similar. The "extraordinary" διαδικασία consisted of a judgement rendered by οἱ φράτερες (lines 13-18), with appeal allowed from them to the Demotionidai (lines 29-44). These groups cannot be identical: either the group which renders the decision in lines 13-18, οἱ φράτερες, is the entire phratry, in which case the Demotionidai is not, or Demotionidai is the phratry, in which case the group which renders the first decision is not. The "regular" διαδικασία consisted of a judgement before the θιασῶται, with appeal allowed from them to "all the *phrateres*." Here there is no ambiguity: θίασοι are groups within the phratry. The appeal is judged by the entire phratry.

If the procedures of the "regular" and "extraordinary" scrutinies are essentially the same, as I have suggested, then the groups involved should also correspond. The Demotionidai should be the same as οἱ ἅπαντες φράτερες: the entire phratry. The group which renders the judgement in lines 13-18, οἱ φράτερες, should be the same as οἱ θιασῶται: a subsection of the phratry.

Wilamowitz provided strong reasons to identify the Demotionidai with οἱ ἅπαντες φράτερες: the Demotionidai judged appeals (line 30); admissions

---

13 The only exception to this generalization which I have encountered is J.H. Lipsius, "Die Phratrie der Demotionidai," *Leipziger Studien* 16 (1894), pp. 161-171.

were regulated by its law (line 13); it had the phratry's registers in its keeping (lines 20-21). Only the *plenum* should have such prerogatives.[14]

The identification of οἱ φράτερες with οἱ θιασῶται, however, is more difficult. Certainly there must be a strong presumption that this group is the same as that which passed the decree (line 9).[15] The decree indisputably was passed by the entire phratry.

Nevertheless, it is possible that οἱ φράτερες does not designate the entire phratry. Five expressions are known to have been used in ancient Athens to describe a subsection of a phratry:[16] ὁ θίασος τοῦ δεῖνος; οἱ θιασῶται τοῦ δεῖνος; οἱ φράτερες τοῦ δεῖνος; οἱ φράτερες μετὰ τοῦ δεῖνος; οἱ οἰκεῖοι τοῦ δεῖνος. The reference to οἱ φράτερες in line 15 is perfectly analogous to the third of these expressions.[17]

There is some indication that a bald, unqualified reference to οἱ φράτερες is insufficient to designate the entire phratry in the context of the description of the διαδικασία. Hierokles refers to "the *phrateres*" only once, at line 15. Nikodemos, however, mentions "the *phrateres*" frequently, but *never* without some qualification. Every time Nikodemos refers to the entire phratry, he distinguishes it from the θιασῶται by calling it οἱ ἅπαντες φράτερες (lines 81, 85, 96, 99, 102). Whenever he contrasts the "rest of the phratry" with the θίασος of the person introduced, he uses the expression οἱ ἄλλοι φράτερες (lines 78, 89, 104). His consistency implies that the phrase

----

[14] Wilamowitz, *AuA* II, p. 261: "Niemand anders als das Plenum kann über die Appelation richten, und die Liste der Brüder ἐν Δημοτιωνιδῶν kann nur im Hause der Bruderschaft liegen. Jede andere Auffassung ist in sich verkehrt."

[15] Wade-Gery, *Demotionidai*, p. 127 argued this point with reference to the implied subject of φέρεν in line 29: "It is inconceivable that the unexpressed subject of φερεν [*sic*] in line 29 can be other than τοσ φρατερασ [*sic*]. Nor will anyone who is familiar with the language of Attic Decrees deny the strong presumption that this is so. The subject of such infinitives is the body which votes the decree." Compare Andrewes, *Philochoros*, p. 4. The argument is just as strong when applied to the φράτερες mentioned in line 15.

[16] Generally on the internal organization of the phratry W.S. Ferguson, "The Athenian Phratries," *CP* 5 (1910), pp. 257-284; A. von Premerstein, "Phratern-Verbände auf einem attischen Hypothekenstein," *Ath. Mit.* 35 (1910), pp. 103-117; Andrewes, *Philochoros.* M. Flower, "*IG* II² 2344 and the Size of Phratries in Classical Athens," *CQ* 35 (1985), pp. 232-235, has recently argued against Premerstein that *IG* II² 2344 is not the list of a θίασος within a phratry, but a complete phratry register. In my opinion he is mistaken in this: see C.W. Hedrick, Jr., "The Phratry from Paiania," *CQ* 59 (1989), pp. 126-135. In addition to *IG* II² 2344 see *IG* II² 2723; 2345; Dem. 57, 43 and 57-69. More recently, consult C.W. Hedrick, Jr., *The Attic Phratry* (Thesis, University of Pennsylvania), Ann Arbor 1984, pp. 143-150.

[17] It must, however, be assumed that there has been an ellipse of the possessive genitive αὐτοῦ in line 15. In Greek, of course, it is not unusual for the possessive genitive to drop out, particularly in passages of a general character. See, *e.g.*, Smyth, *GG* 1199 N.

needs qualification. Evidently the phrase οἱ φράτερες in itself is not an unambiguous designation for the entire phratry. Nikodemos' practice suggests that if Hierokles had wanted to refer to "all the *phrateres*" in line 15, he should have said οἱ ἅπαντες φράτερες.

For these reasons I suggest that the expression οἱ φράτερες in line 15 refers to subsections of the phratry, not to the entire phratry. Some time later Nikodemos consistently uses the term θίασος for such groups. This change in nomenclature is significant. The use of the word θίασος to designate a group within a phratry seems to be an innovation of the late fifth century, imposed on the phratry by the state (see Chapter 3, commentary to line 73). If indeed Hierokles uses the term οἱ φράτερες to refer to a subsection of the phratry, then the change in terminology very likely occurred in the interim between his decree and that of Nikodemos.[18]

The reference in line 15 to οἱ φράτερες is, I suggest, more specifically a reference to οἱ φράτερες αὐτοῦ, that is, to the intimate *phrateres* of the candidate, his θιασῶται. On my interpretation, the procedure of the διαδικασία as described in the decree of Hierokles is perfectly analogous to that of the διαδικασία as described in the decree of Nikodemos. This interpretation makes it possible to identify the Demotionidai as the phratry; most importantly, it provides a consistent reading of the document.

THE HOUSE OF THE DEKELEIANS

The most notorious problem of the document remains to be considered: the identity of the "House of the Dekeleians." As has been shown,[19] there is no evidence for any group in Attica called Δεκελειεῖς with the exception of the members of the deme of Dekeleia. The use of οἶκος as the name of an association is normally derived from the meeting place of the group. It does not necessarily imply that the group is a kinship organization. Three examples of groups which met in οἶκοι were cited: the Chian phratry of the Klytidai, the Attic *genos* of the Kerykes and apparently the demesmen of Melite. In

---

[18] The use of the term θίασος is certainly not introduced in this decree: such a measure would have been mandated by a state decree. Furthermore, as Andrewes points out, "Nikodemos takes their existence for granted" (Andrewes, *Philochoros*, p. 12). It does not follow, however, that these θίασοι had been in existence "for a long time," as Wilamowitz suggested (*AuA* II, p. 263).

[19] See Chapter 3, commentary to line 33.

conclusion I argued that the οἶκος of the Dekeleians took its name from the building in which it met, and might be either a kinship group located in Dekeleia and associated with the phratry of the Demotionidai, or (more probably), that it might consist of the members of the deme itself.

The context in which the group is mentioned in this document furnishes some additional indications of its nature. The οἶκος of the Dekeleians intrudes on the phratry admission procedures at one point only: when appeal is made to the Demotionidai in the "extraordinary" scrutiny. Several features of the procedure have been used to argue the nature and identity of the "House of the Dekeleians": first, the exceedingly steep fine imposed on candidates rejected on appeal; then, the role of the priest of the "House of the Dekeleians"; finally, the part played by the five συνήγοροι from the "House of the Dekeleians" and the oath sworn by them.

The fine of one thousand drachmai imposed on the candidate rejected in the "extraordinary" scrutiny may well seem exorbitant when compared with the other fines mentioned in the decrees of the Demotionidai. The fines are as follows:

THE DECREE OF HIEROKLES

Line 23: If the candidate is rejected by his *phrateres*, then his original sponsor must pay a fine of 100 drachmai.

Line 39: If a candidate appeals an adverse decision to the Demotionidai and is again rejected, then he (that is, the candidate) is liable to a fine of 1,000 drachmai.

Line 49: If the phratriarch does not initiate the procedure of the "extra-ordinary" scrutiny each year, then he is subject to a fine of 500 drachmai.

THE DECREE OF NIKODEMOS

Line 55: If a *phrater* fails to sacrifice on the altar at Dekeleia he is subject to a fine of (50?) drachmai.

Line 91: If the candidate is rejected by the θιασῶται, his introducer apparently pays no fine; if however he is accepted by the θιασῶται and subsequently rejected by the entire phratry, then the θίασος which initially accepted him must pay a fine of 100 drachmai, with the exception of the θιασῶται who openly opposed his admission.

> *Line 99*: If the θιασῶται reject him and the introducer appeals the
> decision to the entire phratry and is there rejected, then the
> introducer must pay a fine of 100 drachmai.

Wade-Gery, holding that the appeal to the Demotionidai was a part of
the "regular" scrutiny, and that the Demotionidai were a privileged aristocratic
group *vis-à-vis* the phratry, maintained that the fine for the rejected candidate
was set so high because he was appealing outside of the phratry. He notes
that everywhere else an adverse decision of the phratry entails a fine of only
one hundred drachmai. He does not attempt to explain the fine of 500
drachmai to which the phratriarch is liable should he not put the vote each
year, since that fine was not provoked by a negative decision of the *phrateres*.

The changes proposed in the outline of the decree of Hierokles allow a
simpler and more reasonable explanation for the large fines prescribed in the
decree of Hierokles: all are exacted from individuals who have unjustly
usurped the rights of a *phrater*. They are meant to be punitive. If a candidate
is rejected by his *phrateres* in the "extraordinary" scrutiny, his original
introducer pays a fine of 100 drachmai. In the "regular" scrutiny, rejection by
the θιασῶται is apparently no cause for a fine. In the appeal to the
Demotionidai, *the candidate* must pay a fine of 1,000 drachmai if he is
rejected. The issue is not the appeal, or the participation of the Demotionidai
or the House of the Dekeleians in the procedure, but the punishment of
someone who has gained admission to the phratry on and enjoyed the rights
of a *phrater* under false pretenses.[20] We may compare the extreme penalties
exacted from an individual who, ejected from his deme in the διαψήφισις, is
rejected on appeal.[21] The fine of five hundred drachmai imposed on the
phratriarch should he fail to initiate the "extraordinary" scrutiny each year
also supports my argument. The fine is set so high because the procedure at
issue is the "extraordinary" scrutiny, and because by not initiating the
procedure the phratriarch would aid and abet the false members of the
phratry.

The fact that the priest of the House of the Dekeleians is charged with
exacting the 1,000 drachmai fine from the rejected appellant is curious. It is
one of the factors which led Wade-Gery to maintain that the name of the

---

[20] J.H. Lipsius, "Die Phratrie der Demotionidai," *Leipziger Studien* 16 (1894), p. 168,
first made this point.

[21] See the comments of P.J. Rhodes, *A Commentary on the Aristotelian Athenaion Politeia*,
Oxford 1981, p. 501.

phratry was the Δεκελειεῖς. He first summarized the activities of the priest(s) in the document, which he grouped into three categories: secretarial duties (lines 2, 19, 60, 66, 107); the administration of oaths (line 32); and the collection of fines (lines 25, 41, 50, 55). His argument consists of the statement that "it seems unlikely that 'the priest' in any of these cases is any other than Theodoros (or his successor), the priest of the phratry."[22] There is, however, the difficulty of the change of nomenclature at line 41. Only here in the document is reference made to the "priest of the House of the Dekeleians." Wade-Gery explained that this is because only here in the document does the full title of the priest *need* to be given. Elsewhere, he remarks, the identity of the priest is apparent, but here "the fine is consequent on a vote of the Demotionidai, but goes to the common treasury; therefore the language is more explicit than usual."[23] Following Wade-Gery's argument, however, one would expect that the same explicitness would be required at line 35, where priest and phratriarch administer the oath to the five συνήγοροι who are to serve at the appeal to the Demotionidai; or at line 20, where priest and phratriarch are to erase the names of those ejected from the list "in the hands of the Demotionidai." It cannot be argued that in these passages the specification is provided by the mention of the phratriarch, for such an argument would raise the same problem in lines 41-42: after the priest of the House of the Dekeleians is ordered to collect the fine, it is allowed that any *phrater* who wishes may also collect. If it is a fair assumption that a new name implies a different office, then the two priests should not be identical. It is true that some[24] have argued that the priest of the phratry is also *de facto* the priest of the House of the Dekeleians. Whether or not this is true, *de jure* the two offices must be distinct.

The House of the Dekeleians appoints five συνήγοροι to look out for *its own interests*.[25] The phratriarch and priest administer an oath to them in which they swear to do their duty justly, and not to permit anyone who is not qualified to enjoy the rights of a *phrater*. It is noteworthy that the oath of the συνήγοροι is administered by the phratriarch and the priest (of the phratry), and that though their oath is quoted, there is no mention of a god by whom they swear, nor apparently do they place their hands on the phratry altar when

---

[22] Wade-Gery, *Demotionidai*, p. 123.

[23] Wade-Gery, *Demotionidai*, p. 128.

[24] For example, Wilamowitz, *AuA*, II, p. 261.

[25] See above, Chapter 3, commentary to line 32.

they swear. This is the only oath cited in the document from which these two requirements have been omitted. As has been seen,[26] the oath is similar, *mutatis mutandis* to that sworn by the συνήγοροι appointed by an Attic deme.

The House of the Dekeleians, then, is a group which had a vested interest in the administration of the "extraordinary" scrutiny, which the Demotionidai had undertaken to expel unqualified members of the phratry. Their interest is evidenced by the συνήγοροι whom they appoint to represent them in the proceedings, and by the fact that their priest is responsible for the collection of the fine from the person expelled, *for the phratry*. It must be kept in mind that the House of the Dekeleians is only involved in the "extraordinary" scrutiny, and seems to have taken no interest in the regular admission of phratry members.

These are the criteria which must be used to identify the "House of the Dekeleians." What group would have had this sort of power and influence over the internal affairs of an Attic phratry? On any interpretation it is clear that the House of the Dekeleians is in a dominant position *vis-a-vis* the Demotionidai. Normally the group has been identified with a *genos*, and has been seen as attesting the survival of an archaic feature of Attic society in the fourth century B.C. Such an interpretation does not explain why the House of the Dekeleians participates only in the "extraordinary" scrutiny, nor does it tell why the priest of a *genos* should collect the fine for a phratry.

In the appeal to the Demotionidai, people who were already in the phratry might be expelled, and in the event that they were rejected on appeal, they, not their introducers, were expected to pay the fine. Once an individual has been expelled, the phratry might find it difficult to collect the fine. In the normal admission procedure, the problem does not arise, for there it is the sponsor who pays the fine, and since he remains in the phratry he dares not be recalcitrant. If he were, the phratry might impose some more serious sanction on him. A person who has been expelled from the phratry can be threatened with no more serious sanctions. Expulsion from a phratry would call into question the individual's qualifications for citizenship. It is natural that the Athenian state should become involved in the process at this point.

It is clear that a correlation existed between phratry membership and deme affiliation. Most *phrateres* were members of the deme in which the phratry shrine was located. The special relationship between deme and phratry is implicitly recognized by a consistent habit of omission: in phratry

---

[26] Chapter 3, commentary to line 36.

documents the demotic is regularly ommitted when a *phrater* belongs to the local deme.[27] The identification of the House of the Dekeleians with the demesmen of Dekeleia clarifies the constitutional relationship between local phratry and deme. When a *phrater* whose membership was at issue appealed to the phratry in the "extraordinary" scrutiny, the deme appointed advocates who took part in the judgement. There is no indication that the deme had veto power over a judgement of the phratry, only that it could plead its own interests. If the individual was rejected on appeal the deme was responsible to collect the fine imposed. The House of the Dekeleians, however, evidently played no part in the "regular" scrutiny. It intervened only when *adults* were to be expelled from the phratry, and hence also from the deme and from the Athenian citizen body. This intervention is natural, given the overlapping concerns of deme and phratry: the determination of the *bona fides* of the Athenian citizen.

This conclusion has far-reaching and obvious implications for our understanding of the classical Athenian constitution and, more particularly, for the reforms of Kleisthenes. Does a deme have general powers to intervene in the affairs of a phratry, or are these powers restricted to situations analogous to that of the "extraordinary" scrutiny? Do these powers date to the time of Kleisthenes, or were they devised to deal with the problems of the citizenship crisis in the wake of the Peloponnesian War? What precisely were the roles of deme and phratry in determining Athenian citizenship? These issues will have to be reconsidered in light of this new interpretation of the Decrees of the Demotionidai.

---

[27] See C.W. Hedrick, Jr., "The Phratry Shrines of Attica and Athens," *Hesperia*, forthcoming.

BIBLIOGRAPHY

ABBREVIATIONS

Andrewes, *Philochoros* = A. Andrewes, "Philochoros on Phratries," *JHS* 81 (1961), pp. 1-15.

Boisacq, *DE* = E. Boisacq, *Dictionnaire étymologique de la langue grècque étudiée dans ses rapports avec les autres langues indo-européennes*, Heidelberg 1907.

Bull. ép. = J. and L. Robert, *Bulletin épigraphique*. An annual review of epigraphical publications appearing in the *REG*. Also issued in separate volumes, Paris 1972-1986. It is cited by the last two digits of the year and the number of the lemma.

Busolt-Swoboda, *Griechische Staatskunde* = G. Busolt and H. Swoboda, *Griechische Staatskunde* (*Handbuch der Altertumswissenschaft* 4, 1), third edition, 2v., Munich 1920-1926.

Davies, *APF* = J.K. Davies, *Athenian Propertied Families*, Oxford 1971.

D-S = C. Daremberg and E. Saglio, *Dictionnaire des antiquités grècques et romaines*, 6v., Paris 1877-1919.

FGrHist = F. Jacoby, *Die Fragmente der griechischen Historiker*, Berlin and Leiden 1923-.

GAInsch[3] = K. Meisterhans and E. Schwyzer, *Grammatik der attischen Inschriften*, third edition, Berlin 1900.

IC = M. Guarducci, ed., *Inscriptiones creticae*, 4v., Rome 1935-1950.

IG = *Inscriptiones graecae*, Berlin 1873-.

IGRRP = R. Cagnat, ed., *Inscriptiones graecae ad res romanas pertinentes*, 4v., Paris 1911-1927.

Kock = T. Kock, *Comicorum atticorum fragmenta*, 3v., Leipzig 1880-1888.

LSJ = H. Liddel, R. Scott and H. Jones, *A Greek-English Lexicon*, with a supplement by E. Barber *et al.*, Oxford 1968.

Olympia, Inschriften = *Olympia, die Ergebnisse der vom deutschen Reich veranstalteten Ausgrabung*, hrsg. von Ernst Curtius und Friedrich Adler, 5v., Berlin 1890-1897. Vol. 5, *Die Inschriften*, von W. Dittenberger und K. Purgold.

PA = J. Kirchner, *Prosopographia Attica*, 2v., Berlin 1901-1903.

Preisigke, *Fachwörterbuch* = F. Preisigke, *Fachwörterbuch des öffentlichen Verwaltungsdienstes Aegyptens in den griechischen Papyruskunden der ptolemaisch-römischen Zeit*, Göttingen 1915.

Preisigke, *Wörterbuch* = F. Preisigke, *Wörterbuch der griechischen Papyruskunden mit Einschluss der griechischen Inschriften, Aufschriften, Ostraka, usw., aus Aegypten*, Berlin 1925-1971.

Prott-Ziehen, *LGS* = H. von Prott and L. Ziehen, eds., *Leges graecorum sacrae e titulis collectae*, 2v., Leipzig 1896-1906.

RE = Pauly-Wissowa, *Real Encylopädie der classischen Altertumswissenschaft*, Stuttgart 1893-1978.

RIJG = R. Dareste, B. Haussouillier, Th. Reinach, *Recueil des inscriptions juridiques grècques*, 2v., Paris 1891-1904.

SEG = *Supplementum epigraphicum graecum*, Leiden 1923-.

SIG = W. Dittenberger, ed., *Sylloge inscriptionum graecarum*, second edition, 3v., Leipzig 1898-1901; third edition, 4v., with supplements by F. Hiller von Gärtringen, 1915-1924.

Schwyzer, *GG* = E. Schwyzer, *Griechische Grammatik, auf der Grundlage von Karl Brugmanns griechischer Grammatik* (*Handbuch der Altertumswissenschaft* 2, 1, 1-4), Munich 1938-1971.

Smyth, *GG* = H. Smyth, *Greek Grammar*, rev. by G. Messing, Cambridge, Mass. 1956.

Sokolowski, *LSA* = F. Sokolowski ed., *Lois sacrées de l'Asie mineure* (*L'école française d'Athènes*, fasc. 9), Paris 1955.

-----, *LSCG* = F. Sokolowski, ed., *Lois sacrées des cités grècques* (*L'école française d'Athènes*, fasc. 18), Paris 1969.

-----, *LSCG, sup.* = F. Sokolowski, ed., *Lois sacrées des cités grècques, supplément* (*L'école française d'Athènes*, fasc. 11), Paris 1962.

Stephanos, *Thesauros* = H. Stephanos and C. Hase, *Thesauros graecae linguae*, third edition, 8v., Paris 1831-1865.

Threatte, *GAI* I = L. Threatte, *The Grammar of Attic Inscriptions*, v.1, New York 1980.

Traill, *POA* = J. Traill, *The Political Organization of Attica: A Study of the Demes, Trittyes and Phylai, and their Representation in the Athenian Council* (*Hesperia* sup. 14), Princeton 1975.

Wade-Gery, *Demotionidai* = H.T. Wade-Gery, "Studies in Attic Society: I. Demotionidai," *CQ* 25 (1931), pp. 129-143 [= *Essays in Greek History*, Oxford 1958, pp. 89-115].

Wilamowitz, *AuA* = U. von Wilamowitz-Möllendorff, *Aristoteles und Athen*, 2v., Berlin 1893.

WORKS CITED

Arvanitopoulou, Th., Δεκελεία (Πολέμων, παράρτημα), Athens 1958.

Arvanitopoulou, Th., with Sophia and Eirene, Princesses of Greece, "Οστρακα ἐκ Δεκελείας, Athens 1959.

Bekker, I., *Anecdota Graeca*, 3v., Berlin 1814-1821.

Bérard, B., *De arbitrio inter liberas graecorum civitates*, Paris 1894.

Bettelheim, B., *Symbolic Wounds: Puberty and the Envious Male*, rev. edition, New York 1962.

Bizos: see Gernet and Bizos.

Bourriot, F., *Récherches sur la nature du génos: étude d'histoire sociale Atheniènne-- périodes archaique et classique*, Lille 1976.

Caillemer, E., "Διαδικασία," in D-S 2, 1 (1892), p. 122.

Chantraine, P., *Dictionnaire étymologique de la langue grècque, histoire des mots*, 4v., Paris 1968-1980.

Crosby, M., "The Leases of the Laurion Mines," *Hesperia* 19 (1950), pp. 189-312.

De Schutter, X., "Le culte d'Apollon Patrôos à Athènes," *AC* 56 (1987), pp. 103-129.

Deubner, L., *Attische Feste*, Berlin 1932.

Dindorff, G., ed., *Iulii Pollucis onomasticon*, 5v., Leipzig 1824.

Dow, S., "The List of Athenian Archontes," *Hesperia* 3 (1934), pp. 140-190.

-----, "The Purported Decree of Themistokles, Stele and Inscription," *AJA* 66 (1962), pp. 354-368.

Edmonds, J., *The Fragments of Attic Comedy*, 3v., Leiden 1957-1961.

Eitrem, S., "Die Labyadai und die Byzyga," *Eranos* 20 (1921-1922), pp. 91-121.

Ferguson, W.S., "The Athenian Phratries," *CP* 5 (1910), pp. 257-284.

-----, "The Salaminioi of Heptaphyle and Sounion," *Hesperia* 7 (1938), pp. 1-74.

-----, "The Attic Orgeones," *HThR* 37 (1944), pp. 61-140.

Flower, M.A., "*IG* II^2 2344 and the Size of Phratries in Classical Athens," *CQ* 35 (1985), pp. 232-235.

Fränkel, E., *RE* 16, 2 (1935), Namenwesen, cols. 1611-1670.

Frisk, H., *Griechisches etymologisches Wörterbuch*, 2v., Heidelberg 1960-1970.

Gernet, L., and M. Bizos, eds., *Lysias*, Paris 1924-1926.

Gilbert, G., "Der Beschluss der Phratrie der Demotionidai," *JbPh* 135 (1887), pp. 23-28.

-----, *Greek Constitutional Antiquities* (English translation of the 1893 edition of his *Griechischen Staatsalterthümer*), London 1895.

Gluskina, L.M., "Phratry and Clan in Fourth Century Athens," *VDI* 165 (1983), pp. 39-52.

Golden, M., "Demosthenes and the Age of Majority in Athens," *Phoenix* 33 (1979), pp. 25-38.

Gradenwitz, O., *Zum Falscheid des P. Halensis 1 (Dikaiomata)*, (*SHAW* 6, no. 8), Heidelberg 1913.

Graeca Halensis, *Dikaiomata*, Berlin 1913.

Guarducci, M., "L'istituzione della fratria nella Grecia antica e nelle colonie greche di Italia," parte prima, *MAL* ser. 6, 6 (1937), pp. 5-101; parte secunda, *MAL* ser. 6, 8 (1938), pp. 65-135.

Harrison, A.R.W., *The Law of Athens*, 2v., Oxford 1968-1971.

Haussoullier, B., *La vie municipale en Attique; essai sur l'organisation des dèmes au quatrième siècle* (*Librairie des écoles françaises d'Athènes et de Rome*), Paris 1884.

Hedrick, C.W., Jr., "Old and New on the Attic Phratry of the Therrikleidai," *Hesperia* 52 (1983), pp. 299-302.

-----, *The Attic Phratry* (Thesis, University of Pennsylvania), Ann Arbor 1984.

-----, "The Temple and Cult of Apollo Patroos in Athens," *AJA* 92 (1988), pp. 185-210.

-----, "An Honorific Phratry Inscription," *AJP* 109 (1988), pp. 111-117.

-----, "The Thymaitian Phratry," *Hesperia* 57 (1988), pp. 81-85.

-----, "The Phratry from Paiania," *CQ* 59 (1989), pp. 129-135.

-----, "The Phratry Shrines of Attica and Athens," *Hesperia*, forthcoming.

Höfer, U., *RL* 3, 2 (1902-1909), Φράτριοι, cols. 2454-2457.

Honigmann, E., *RE* 15, 1 (1931), Melite no. 9, cols. 541-542.

Humphreys, S., *Anthropology and the Greeks*, London 1978.

Ito, Sadao, "An Interpretation of the so-called Demotionid Inscription," *The Journal of History* (Kyoto) 71 (1988), pp. 677-713.

Jacoby, F., *Atthis: the Local Chronicles of Ancient Athens*, Oxford 1949.

Just, M., *Die Ephesis in der Geschichte des attischen Prozesses-- ein Versuch zur Deutung der Rechtsnatur der Ephesis* (Thesis Würzburg), Würzburg 1965.

Keramopoulos, A., "Τὸ Βουλευτήριον τῶν Τεχνιτῶν ἐν᾽Αθήναις," *AD* 11 (1927-1928), pp. 111-122.

Kirchner, J., *RE* 21, 1 (1941), Phormion no. 3, col. 537.

Klaffenbach, G., *Bemerkungen zum griechischen Urkundenwesen* (*SDAW* no. 6), Berlin 1960.

Körte, A., "Mitgliederverzeichnis einer attischen Phratrie," *Hermes* 37 (1902), pp. 582-589.

Koumanoudes, S., "Ψήφισμα Φρατερικόν," *ArchEph* (1883), cols. 69-76.

Krummrey, H. and S. Panciera, "Criteri de edizione e segni diacritici," *Tituli* 2 (1980), pp. 205-215.

Kyparissis, N., and H. A. Thompson, "A Sanctuary of Zeus and Athena Phratrios Newly Found in Athens," *Hesperia* 7 (1938), pp. 612-625.

Labarbe, J., "L'age corréspondant au sacrifice du κούρειον et les données historiques du sixième discours d'Isée," *BAB* 39 (1953), pp. 358-394.

Lacey, W.K., *The Family in Classical Greece*, Ithaca 1968.

Lambert, S., *The Ionian Phyle and Phratry in Archaic and Classical Athens* (Thesis, Oxford), Ann Arbor 1986.

Larfeld, W., *Handbuch der griechischen Epigraphie*, 2v., Leipzig 1898-1907.

Latte, K., *RE* 20, 1 (1941), φρατρίαρχος, cols. 745-746.

-----, *RE* 20, 1 (1941), phratrie, cols. 746-756.

-----, *RE* 20, 1 (1941), φράτριοι θεοί, cols. 756-758.

Ledl, A., "Das attische Bürgerrecht und die Frauen," *WS* 29 (1907), pp. 173-227; 30 (1908), pp. 1-46, 173-230.

Leist, G., *Der attische Eigentümerstreit im System der Diadikasien* (Tübinger Inauguraldissertation), Jena 1886.

Lewis, D., "Notes on Attic Inscriptions (II)," *ABS(A)* 50 (1955), pp. 1-36.

Lipsius, J.H., "Die Phratrie der Demotionidai," *Leipziger Studien* 16 (1894), pp. 161-171.

-----, *Das attische Recht und Rechtsverfahren*, 3v., Leipzig 1905-1915.

Lolling, H., "Ἀνασκαφαὶ καὶ εὑρήματα ἐν Δεκελείᾳ," *AD* 4 (1888), pp. 159-163.

MacDowell, D.M., ed., *Aristophanes, Wasps*, Oxford 1971.

-----, *The Law in Classical Athens*, London 1978.

Maier, F., *Griechischen Mauerbauinschriften*, 2v., Heidelberg 1959-1961.

Mare, W., *A Study of the Greek* ΒΩΜΟΣ *in Classical Greek Literature* (Thesis, University of Pennsylvania), Philadelphia 1961.

Meritt, B.D., "Greek Inscriptions," *Hesperia* 30 (1961), pp. 205-292.

Milchhöfer, A., "Antikenbericht aus Attika," *Ath. Mit.* 12 (1887), pp. 277-330.

-----, *RE* 4, 2 (1901), Dekeleia, col. 2425.

Mikalson, J.D., *The Sacred and Civic Calendar of the Athenian Year*, Princeton 1975.

Mommsen, A., *Heortologie, antiquarische Untersuchungen über die städtischen Feste der Athener*, Leipzig 1864.

-----, *Feste der Stadt Athen*, Leipzig 1898.

Müller, O., "Untersuchungen zur Geschichte des attische Bürger- und Eherechts," *Jahrbücher für Classischen Philologie*, supplementband 25 (1899), pp. 661-865.

Nilsson, M.P., *Cults, Myths, Oracles and Politics in Ancient Greece*, 1951 (reprint New York 1972).

Panciera, S.: see Krummrey and Panciera.

Pantazides, J., "'Ἐπιγραφὴ ἐκ Δεκελείας," *ArchEph* (1888), cols. 1-20.

Parke, H.W., *Festivals of the Athenians*, London 1977.

Paton, W. R., "Comment on Tarbell's 'Study of an Attic Phratry,' " *AJA* 6 (1890), pp. 314-318.

-----, "The Decelean Inscription and Attic Phratries," *CR* 5 (1891), pp. 221-223.

Patterson, C., *Perikles' Citizenship Law of 451/0 B.C.*, Salem 1981.

Poland, F., *Geschichte des griechischen Vereinswesens* (*Gekrönte Preisschrift* 38), Leipzig 1909.

Premerstein, A. von, "Phratern-Verbände auf einem attischen Hypothekenstein," *Ath. Mit.* 35 (1910), pp. 103-117.

Reisch, E., *RE* 1, 2 (1894), Altar, cols. 1640-1691.

Rhodes, P.J., *The Athenian Boule*, Oxford 1972.

-----, *A Commentary on the Aristotelian Athenaion Politeia*, Oxford 1981.

Robert, L., *Collection Froehner*, Paris 1936.

-----, "Communication: épigraphie et paléographie," *CRAI* (1955), pp. 195-222.

-----, "Inscriptions d'Athènes et de la Grèce centrale," *ArchEph* (1966), pp. 7-19.

-----, "Les épigrammes satiriques de Lucillius," in *L'épigramme grècque* (*Fondation Hardt* 14), Geneva 1969, pp. 179-295.

Roussel, D., *Tribu et cité* (*Annales littéraires de l'Université de Besançon*, v. 193), Paris 1976.

Ruschenbusch, E., ΣΟΛΩΝΟΣ ΝΟΜΟΙ (*Historia Einzelschrift*, heft 9), Wiesbaden 1966.

-----, "Die Diaitetenliste *IG* II/III^2 1927," *ZPE* 49 (1982), pp. 267-281.

Ste. Croix, G.E.M. de, *The Origins of the Peloponnesian War*, Ithaca 1972.

Sauppe, H., "Commentatio de phratriis," *Index scholarum in Academia Georgia Augusta*, 1886.

-----, "Commentatio de phratriis altera," *Index scholarum in Academia Georgia Augusta*, 1890.

Schäfer, C., *Altes und Neues über die attischen Phratrie*, Naumberg 1888.

Schöll, R., "Die kleisthenischen Phratrien," *SBAW* (1889), part 2, pp. 1-25.

-----, *RE* 5 (1905), Demotionidai, cols. 194-202.

Sealey, R., *The Athenian Republic: Democracy or the Rule of Law?*, University Park 1987.

Shear, T.L., Jr., "The Athenian Agora, Excavation of 1980-1982," *Hesperia* 33 (1984), pp. 1-57.

Stengel, P., *Die griechischen Kultusaltertümer* (*Handbuch der Altertumswissenschaft* 5, 3), Munich 1920.

Szanto, E., "Zur attischen Phratrien- und Geschlechter-verfassung," *RhM* 40 (1885), pp. 506-520.

Tarbell, F. B., "The Decrees of the Demotionidai, a Study of the Attic Phratry," *AJA* 5 (1889), pp. 135-153 [=*Papers of the American School in Athens* 5 (1886-1890), pp. 170-188].

-----, "Mr. Tarbell's Reply to Mr. Paton's Comment," *AJA* 6 (1890), pp. 318-320.

Thompson, H.A., "Buildings on the West Side of the Agora," *Hesperia* 6 (1937), pp. 1-222.

Thompson: see Kyparissis and Thompson.

Thompson, W.E., "An Interpretation of the 'Demotionid' Decrees," *SO* 62 (1968), pp. 51-68.

Thür, G., "Kannte das altgriechische Recht die Eigentums-diadikasie?" *Symposion 1977. Vorträge zur griechischen und hellenistischen Rechtsdienst* (*Akten der Gesellschaft für griechische und hellenistische Rechtsgeschichte*, bd. 3), Köln 1982.

Töpffer, J., *Attische Genealogie*, Berlin 1889 (Reprint New York, 1973).

-----, *RE* 1 (1894), Apatouria, cols. 2672-2680.

Van Gennep, A., *The Rites of Passage*, trans. M. Vizedom and G. Caffee, reprint Chicago 1960.

Vidal-Naquet, P., *The Black Hunter: Forms of Thought and Forms of Society in the Greek World*, trans. A. Szegedy-Maszak, Baltimore 1986.

-----, "The Black Hunter Revisited," *PCPS* 212 n.s. 32 (1986), pp. 126-144.

Walbank, M., "Greek Inscriptions from the Athenian Agora, Fifth to Third Centuries B.C.," *Hesperia* 51 (1982), pp. 41-56.

Wehrli, F., *Die Schule des Aristoteles*, 10v., Basel 1944-1959.

Whitehead, D., *The Demes of Attica, 508/7-ca. 250 B.C.: A Political and Social Study*, Princeton 1986.

Wilhelm, A., "Zu griechischen Inschriften," *AEMOe* 20 (1897), pp. 50-97.

-----, "Ἀττικὰ Ψηφίσματα," *ArchEph* (1905), 217-281.

-----, *Beiträge zur griechischen Inschriftenkunde (Sonderschriften des OeAI in Wien*, bd. 7), Vienna 1909.

-----, *Attische Urkunden (SAWW* 180, 217, 220), Vienna 1916-1942.

Willemsen, F., "Vom Grabbezirk des Nikodemos in Dekeleia," *MDAI(A)* 89 (1974), pp. 173-191.

Wycherley, R., *Literary and Epigraphical Testimonia (Athenian Agora* v.3), Princeton 1957.

Ziebarth, E., *Das griechisches Vereinswesen*, Stuttgart 1896.

INDICES

INDEX TO THE INSCRIPTION

All numbers in this index refer to the line numbers of the "decrees of the Demotionidai, the text of which is published in Chapter 2.

ἀγαθός: 112
ἀγορά: 86
ἄγω: 52, 60, 119
Ἀθηναῖοι: 10-11
αἱρέομαι: 32
ἀληθής: 111
ἄλλος: 68, 115; ὁ βουλόμενος: 43, 51; φράτερες: 78, 89-90, 104
ἀναγορεύω: 87
ἀναγράφω: 2-3, 65-66, 122, 124, 125-126
ἀνάκρισις: 72
ἀνήρ: 33
ἀντίγραφον: 21-22
ἅπαντες: φράτερες: 81, 85, 96, 96-97, 99, 102
'Ἀπατούρια: 28-29
ἀπογράφω: 117-118, 121-122
ἀποδικάζω: 22
ἀποψηφίζομαι: 31, 38-39, 90, 95, 98-99, 101
ἀποψήφισις: 102-103
ἀργύριον: 6, 8, 24-25, 41, 51, 57
ἀριθμός: 77
ἄρχω: 10, 45
ἄστυ: 64
αὐτίκα: 16

βούλομαι: 30, 43, 51
βωμός: 18, 29, 54 (bis), 67, 76, 83

γαμετή: 110-111
γίγνομαι: 34
γνήσιος: 110
γραμματεῖον: 20-21; plural: 98

δεῖ: 47
Δεκελεία: 53, 67, 122-123
Δεκελειεῖς: 63-64; οἶκος Δ.: 33, 42
Δημοτιωνίδαι: 14-15, 21, 30-31, 39
δῆμος: 119, 120
διαδικάζω: present active: 47; aorist

active 15; aorist passive: 13-14
διαδικασία: 26, 70-71, 79, 94
διακωλύω: 59
διαριθμέω: 86-87
διαψηφίζομαι: 83-84
δίδωμι: 4; τὴν ψῆφον: 80
δίκαιος: 36
δοκέω: 9, 18, 97, 114
Δορπία: 62
δραχμή: 23, 39-40, 49, 55, 91, 99-100

ἐάω: 37
ἐγγράφω: 97
εἰμί: 27, 45, 76, 79, 102, 112-113; φράτηρ: 18, 37, 89, 97
εἶπον: 13, 68, 114
ἔρομαι: 71-72
εἰσάγω: present active: 95-96, 109; present middle: 82, 117; aorist active: 22; aorist passive: 18-19
εἰσαγωγή: 70, 108-109, 115
εἰσπράττω: 24, 40-41, 44, 50, 56
ἕκαστος: 48
ἑκατόν: 23, 91, 99
ἐκτίθημι: 122, 123
ἐλατήρ: 7
ἔλατον: 63
ἐναντίος: 84-85, 113
ἐναντιόω: 93
ἐνιαυτόν: 47
ἐνταῦθα: 60
ἐξαλείφω: 19
ἔξεστι: 31, 42-43
ἐξορκέω: 35
ἐπιορκέω: 113
ἐπιψηφίζομαι: 45-46, 48
ἐπόμνυμι: 74, 75-76
ἔτος: 27, 34, 118
εὐορκέω: 112
Εὐφαντίδης: 2
ἐφίημι: 30, 38, 96, 101-102

ἔχομαι: 76

Ζεύς Φράτριος: 1, 16-17, 23, 40, 49, 56, 74, 91, 100, 111

ἥμιχος: 8

Θεόδωρος Εὐφαντίδου: 2
θίασος: 77, 105
θιασῶται: 73, 82, 88-89, 92, 93, 95, 101, 103 (bis)
θύω: 28, 54

ἱερεύς: 2, 4, 19-20, 25, 35-36, 50, 56-57, 59-60, 66, 107, 123, 126; Δεκελειῶν οἴκου: 41
ἱερεώσυνα: 4, 65
Ἱεροκλῆς: 13
ἱερόν, τό: τῆς Λητοῦς: 124-125
ἱερός: δραχμαί: 23, 40, 49, 55, 91, 100
ἵστημι: 3

κατήγορος: 93
κεῖμαι: 69
κοινόν, τό: 44, 52
κοινός: γραμματεῖα: 98
κούρειον: 6, 28, 118-119; plural: 53, 61
Κουρεῶτις: 28
κρύβδην: 82
κύριος: 102

λευκός: 124
λεύκω: 62-63
Λητώ: 125
λίθινος: 66, 107-108, 126
λοιπόν: 27, 52

μάλα: 16
μάρτυρ: 71, 75, 108
μαρτυρέω: 73, 75, 109
μεῖον: 5; plural: 53, 60-61
μέλλω: 117
Μενέξενος: 114
μήπω: 13
μήτηρ: 120

Νικόδημος: 68
νόμος: 14

ὅδε: 4-5, 9, 65
οἶδα: 116
οἶκος Δεκελειῶν: 33, 42
οἶνος: 8
Οἶον (Δεκελεικόν): 12

ὄνομα: 19, 119
ὅποι: 59
ὁπόσος: 13
ὁπότερος: 87
ὅπου: 63, 122
ὅρκος: 108
ὅσος: 92
οὐδείς: 37
οὗτος: 25, 34, 41, 44-45, 52, 57, 59, 77, 84, 110, 111
οὕς: 5-6, 7
ὀφέλλω: 22-23, 26, 39, 42, 48-49, 54-55, 57-58, 90-91, 99

παῖς: 70, 80-81, 105, 109, 115
Παντακλῆς ἐξ Οἴου: 11-12
πάρειμι: 85-86
παρέχομαι: 72, 78
πατρόθεν: 119, 120
πέντε: 33
πεντακόσιοι: 49
πεντήκοντα: 55
πινακίον: 62
πλευρόν: 5, 7
πλήν: 92
πολύς: 112
πρίν: 81
προγράφω: 60, 61
προπέμπτα: 61-62
προσαναγράφω: 106-107
πρόσθεν: 66-67
προσφοιτάω: 64, 123
πρότερος: 69, 79-80, 116
πρῶτος: 118

σανίδιον: 124
σπιθαμιαῖον: 63
στήλη: 3, 66, 107, 126
συνηγορέω: 36
συνήγορος: 32

τέλος: 67
τοσοῦτος: 77
τρεῖς: 71
τριάκοντα: 34

ὑός: 110
ὑπερωτάω: 73
ὑπισχνέομαι: 16
ὕστερος: 27

φαίνομαι: 94
φέρω: τὴν ψῆφον: 17, 29, 83, 104
Φορμίων: 10, 45

φρατερικός: 125
φράτηρ: 9, 15-16, 44, 78, 114, 117; ἄλλοι:
    90, 104; ἄπαντες: 81, 85; εἶναι: 18,
    37, 89, 97
φρατριαρχέω: 11
φρατρίαρχος: 20, 25-26, 35, 46, 79, 86, 121
    (bis)
φρατρίζω: 37-38
Φράτριος: see Ζεύς

χιλίοι: 39
χοινικιαῖος: 7-8
ψηφίζομαι: 88 (bis)
ψήφισμα: 65, 69, 106, 116, 125
ψῆφος: 17, 29, 80, 83, 84, 105

INDEX OF MODERN AUTHORS

Andrewes, A.: 48 n.130, 57 n.164, 57-58, 57 nn.166-168, 58 n.170, 77 n.12, 79 n.16, 80 n.18
Arvanitopoulou, Th.: viii, 1 n.1, 2-3, 2 nn. 6-7 and 9, 3 nn.10-11, 6

Bekker, I.: 50 n.142
Bérard, B.: 38 n.101, 39 n.103
Bettelheim, B.: 29 n.41
Bizos, M.: 47 n.125
Bourriot, F.: 77 n.12
Busolt, G.: 36 n.89, 77 n.10

Caillemer, E.: 34 n.69
Chantraine, P.: 34 n.70, 38 n.101
Crosby, M.: 25, 25 n.15

Davies, J.K.: 24, 24 nn.11 and 14, 59 n.176
Dareste, R.: see Index Locorum, RIJG
De Schutter, X.: 20 n.2
Deubner, L.: 42 n.108
Dindorff, G.: 27 n.28
Dow, S.: 53 n.153

Edmonds, J.: 27 n.29
Eirene, Princess of Greece: see Arvanitopoulou
Eitrem, S.: 42 n.108

Ferguson, W.S.: 57 nn.163-164 and 167, 79 n.16
Flower, M.: 20 n.1, 79 n.16
Fränkel, E.: 23 n.8
Frisk, H.: 27 n.27, 39 n.101
Gärtringen, F. Hiller von: see Index Locorum, SIG³
Gernet, L.: 47 n.125
Gilbert, G.: 76 n.6
Golden, M.: 28 n.31, 57 n.165
Gluskina, L.M.: 77 n.12
Gradenwitz, O.: 38 n.101
Graeca Halensis: 38 n.101
Guarducci, M.: vii n.1, 40 n.104, 50 n.140, 59 n.179, 77 n.12

Harrison, A.R.W.: 33 n.68, 34 n.69, 42 n.109, 44 n.116, 57 n.161
Haussouillier, B.: 35 n.76; see Index Locorum, RIJG
Hedrick, C.W., Jr.: viii n.3, ix n.6, 11, 20 nn.1-2, 21 n.6, 22 n.7, 23 nn.8 and 10, 26 nn.20 and 22, 28 n.35, 30 nn.45 and 47, 31 nn.55 and 58-59, 32 n.65,

37 n.92, 42 n.108, 60 n.185, 67 n.13, 79 n.16, 85 n.27
Höfer, U.: 20 n.2
Honigmann, E.: 51 n.145
Humphreys, S.C.: 77 n.12

Ito, Sadao: 77 n.12

Jacoby, F.: vii n.1, 35 n.76
Just, M.: 43 n.109, 77 n.12

Keramopoulos, A.: 51 n.145
Kirchner, J.: 31 n.51, 59 n.174
Klaffenbach, G.: 38 nn.97-98
Köhler, U: 1, 6, 10-11, 75 n.2; see Index Locorum, IG II
Körte, A.: 27 n.30
Koumanoudes, S: 1, 1 nn.1-2, 6, 10, 75 n.2
Krummrey, H.: 7 n.1
Kyparissis, N.: 37 n.92

Labarbe, J.: 26 nn.22 and 25, 28 nn.31-32 and 36, 29 nn.39 and 41, 42 n.108, 59 n.178
Lacey, W.K.: 23 n.10, 49 n.134
Lambert, S.D.: 77 n.12
Larfeld, W.: 30 n.46, 56 n.160
Latte, K.: 20 n.2, 29 n.38, 31 nn.57-58
Ledl, A.: 28 n.36, 29 n.37
Leist, G.: 33 n.68, 34 n.69
Lewis, D.: 25 n.16
Lipsius, J.H.: 33 n.68, 34 n.69, 38 nn.101-102, 53 n. 151, 60 n.182, 62 n.3, 70 n.15, 77 n.8, 78 n.13, 82 n.20
Lolling, H: 1-2, 1 nn.1 and 3, 2 n.4, 6, 11

MacDowell, D.M.: 43 n.114, 44 n.116
Maier, F.: 50 n.138
Mare, W.: 37 nn. 90-91
Meritt, B.D.: 49 n.135
Mikalson, J.D.: 42 n.108
Milchhöfer, A.: 6, 45 n.119, 47 n.127
Mommsen, A.: 27 n.26, 42 n.108
Müller, O.: 29 n.37
Münter, L.: 1

Nilsson, M.P.: 42 n.108, 77 n.12

Panciera, S.: 7 n.1
Pantazides, J: 1-2, 2 n.5, 6, 10-11, 76 n.9
Parke, H.W.: 42 n.108
Paton, W.R.: 6, 10, 75 n.4
Patterson, C.: 54 n.154

Poland, F.: 48 nn.128-129, 57 n.163
Preisigke, F.: 38 n.101
Premerstein, A. von: 79 n.16
Prott, H. von: see Index Locorum, *LGS*

Reinach, Th.: see Index Locorum, *RIJG*
Reisch, E.: 37 n.91
Rhodes, P.: vii n.1, 31 n.50, 35 n.76, 43
    nn.110 and 115, 54 n.154, 65 n.9, 82
    n.21
Robert, L.: 25 n.18, 48 n.128, 49 nn.135-
    137, 59 n.177
Roussel, D.: 77 n.12
Ruschenbusch, E.: 25 n.16, 36 n.89

Ste. Croix, G.E.M. de: 52 n.146
Sauppe, H.: 6, 10, 54, 76, 76 n.6
Schäffer, C.: 76, 76 n.5, 77 n.12
Schöll, R.: 45 n.122, 50 n.141, 53 n.151,
    59 nn.179-180, 70 n.15, 75 n.4, 76 n.8,
    77 n.12
Schwyzer, E.: 38 n.97, 53 n.152
Sealey, R.: 28 n.31, 48 n.128
Shear, T.L., Jr.: 55 n.156
Smythe, H.W.: 36 n.83, 52 n.150, 53
    nn.151-152, 79 n.17
Sokolowski, F.: see Index Locorum, *LSA,
    LSCG*
Sophia, Princess of Greece: see Arvani-
    topoulou
Stengel, P.: 23 n.9
Stephanos, H.: 38 n.101
Swoboda, H.: 36 n.89, 77 n.10
Szanto, E.: 75-76, 75 nn.1 and 3-4

Tarbell, F.B.: 6, 38 n.102, 76 n.7, 77 n.12
Thompson, H.A.: 37 n.92
Thompson, W.E.: 35-36, 35 nn.76-77 and
    79-82, 65 n.10, 77 n.12
Threatte, L.: 25 n.19, 28 n.33, 59 n.173
Thür, G.: 34 nn. 70-73
Töpffer, J.: 42 n.108, 45 nn.120 and 122
Traill, J.: 36 n.87

Van Gennep, A.: 29 n.41
Vidal-Naquet, P.: 29 n.41, 42 n.108

Wade-Gery, H.T.: 35, 35 n.78, 38 n.102,
    43-44, 43 nn. nn.112-113, 43 n.115, 44
    n.117, 45 n.122, 46 n.123, 47-48, 47
    n.126, 52 n.148, 55 n.157, 62 n.2, 64
    n.6, 66 n.12, 70, 70 n.16, 71-72, 71
    n.18, 77, 77 nn.11-12, 79 n.15, 82-83,
    83 nn.22-23
Walbank, M.: 21 n.6, 26 n.20
Wehrli, F.: vii n.1
Whitehead, D.: 35 n.76
Wilamowitz-Möllendorff, U. von: 31 n.58,
    36, 36 n.86, 38 n.102, 43-44, 43 n.111,

48, 48 nn.130-132, 62 n.2, 66 n.12, 72
    n.19, 76, 76 n.9, 77 n.12, 78-79, 79
    n.14, 80 n.18, 83 n.24
Wilhelm, A.: 20 n.1, 21 n.5, 38 nn.97 and
    99 and 101, 41 n.105, 48 n.128
Willemsen, F.: 3 n.12, 55 n.158
Wycherley, R.: 54 n.155

Ziebarth, E.: 49 n.137
Ziehen, L.: see Index Locorum, LGS

INDEX LOCORUM

Aesch. = Aeschines
2
    147: 37 n.92

Ameipsias
    F. 7 (Edmonds): 27 n.29

Andocides
1
    126: 28 n.34, 37 n.92

Antiphon
6
    47: 39

Aristophanes
   Acharnians
    146: 28 n.36
   Frogs
    797-798: 27 n.26
   Knights
    1181: 29 n.43
   Fragments
    F. 115 (Kock): 51 n.144
    F. 286 (Edmonds): 27 n.26

Aristotle
   Ath. Pol
    F. 5 Opp.: vii n.1
   Politics
    1268 b, 2, 9: 39-40

Athenaios
2
    57a: 29 n.43
5
    185c: 57 n.164
8
    368: 27 n.29

Bekker, *Anecdota Graeca*
I
    p. 281 line 25: 50 n.142

Dem. = Demosthenes
18
    134: 37 n.90
39
    4: 37 n.95
    20-21: 37 n.93
    29-30: 37 n.94, 37 n.95
40
    11: 37 n.95

43
    11-15: 21 n.3, 28 n.34, 37 nn.92
      and 94, 37 n.95, 49 n.134,
      52 n.150
    81-83: 21 n.3, 28 n.34, 37 nn.92
      and 94
44
    4: 38 n.96
    41: 37 n.94, 60 n.184
57
    9-13: 35 n.76
    23-25: 31 nn.54 and 56
    43: 37 n.94, 79 n.16
    46: 37 n.95
    57-69: 37 n.95, 79 n.16
59
    13: 37 n.93
    55: 37 n.93
    59: 37 n.94
    118: 37 n.93

Digest
47
    22, 4: 36 n.89

Dikaiarchos
   FGrHist 228 gen.: vii n.1
   F. 52 (Wehrli): vii n. 1

Diodoros
11
    60: 36 n.88
14
    54: 31 n.51

Diogenes Laertius
1
    71: 40

Etymologicum Magnum, *s.vv.*
    Ἀπατούρια: 26 n.22
    κούρεον: 26 n.23
    Κουρεῶτις: 26 n.24, 27 n.26
    Μελιτέων οἶκος: 50 n.143
    φράτορες: 31 n.58, 52 n.150

Harp. = Harpokration, *s.vv.*
    μεῖον: 26 n.24
    θίασος: 57 n.163
    φράτερες: 31 n.58

Herodotus
  9
      73: 45-46, 46 n.124, 47 n.127
      74: 46 n.124

Hesperia
  6 (1937)
      pp. 104-107: 37 n.92
  7 (1938)
      pp. 615-619: 37 n.92
  19 (1950)
      pp. 189-312, no. 21: 25 n.15
  30 (1961)
      pp. 229-30, no. 28-29: 49 n.135
  51 (1982)
      pp. 41-56, no. 7: 26 n.20
  52 (1983)
      pp. 299-302: 26 n.20

Hesychios, *s.vv.*
      ἐλατήρ: 29 n.43
      Κουρεῶτις: 29 n.40
      Μελιτέων οἶκος: 50-51

Hyperides
  3
      31: 36 n.88

Hypothesis Aristophanes Wasps
      15-17: 40

IC
  IV
      22b: 39

IG
  I³
      4: 31 n.50, 53 n.152
      105: 31 n.50

  II
      2 (addenda), 841 b: 6
      5, 841 b: 6

  II²
      114: 31 n.50
      1180: 52 n.146
      1183: 52 n.147
      1238: 30 n.47, 31 n.53
      1239: 21 n.3, 31 n.54, 32 n.60
      1240: 21 n.5, 22 n.7, 26 n.21, 32 n.60
      1241: 30 n.49, 31 nn.52 and 55, 32 nn.60-63, 45 n.121, 50 n.139
      1604: 24 n.13
      1672: 50 n.138
      1927: 25 n.16

      2343: 57 n.165
      2344: 20 n.1, 23 n.8, 79 n.16
      2345: 57 n.165, 79 n.16
      2346: 57 n.165
      2347: 57 n.165
      2348: 57 n.165
      2622: 50 n.139
      2625: 36 n.88
      2723: 79 n.16
      2725: 25 n.17
      5156: 60 n.183
      5980a: 55 n.158
      5980b: 55 n.158
      5983: 55 n.158
      10607: 55 n.158
      12865: 55 n.158, 56 n.159

  XII, 9
      1242: 36 n.88

IGRRP
  I
      610: 49 n.137
  III
      14: 49 n.137

Isaios
  2
      14-17: 37 n.93
  3
      73-76: 36 n.89, 37 n.95
      79-80: 37 n.95
  6
      10-11: 37 nn.94-95
      21-26: 28 n.34
  7
      13-17: 28 n.34, 36 n.89, 37 nn.92-93, 38 n.96, 43 n.110, 60 n.184
      26-27: 38 n.96
  8
      18-20: 28 n.34, 36 n.89, 37 n.93
  10
      8-9: 37 n.94
      15: 37 nn.94-95
      21: 37 n.94

Isocrates
  8
      88: 60 n.184

Krateros
  FGrHist 342
      F.4: 52 n.150

Kritias
      F.71 D: 39

LGS
   II
      no. 17: 27 nn.29 and 30, 29 n.43

LSA
      no. 39: 29 nn.38 and 42

LSCG
      no. 19: 27 nn.29 and 30, 29 n.43
      no. 20: 30 n.44

Lysias
   23
      2: 46-47, 47 n.125, 47 n.127, 54
         n.155

Olympia, Inschriften
      2: 20 n.1

P. Gurob.
      2: 40

P. Hal.
      1: 40

P. Oxy.
   31
      2538: 37 n.95

P. Petr.
      21a: 40

Philochoros
   FGrHist 328
      F. 35: vii n.2
      F. 94: vii n.2, 32 n.66

Photios, *s.vv.*
      μειαγωγός: 26 n.24, 27 n.26
      μεῖον: 26 n.24, 27 n.26

Pindar
   Isthmian
      6, 63-65: 48 n.133

Plato Comicus
      F. 213 (Kock): 51 n.144

Pollux
   1
      24: 20 n.2
   3
      51: 20 n.2, 27 n.26
      51-53: 26 n.24, 30 n.45
      52: 29 n.42
   6
      22: 30 n.45

   8
      9: 40
      107: 28 n.32

Polyainos
   3
      9, 15: 40

Plutarch
   Themistokles
      17: 37 n.90
   Perikles
      32: 37 n.90

RIJG
   II
      no. 29: ix n.5, 34 nn.74-75, 38
         n.102, 45 nn.120 and 122,
         48 n.132, 55 n.157, 57
         n.162, 60 n.181, 70 n.15

Robert, *Collection Froehner*
      no. 8: 49 n.135

Scholia (Aristophanes)
   Frogs
      798: 26 n.24, 27 nn.26 and 28,
         28 n.36
   Knights
      1181: 29 n.43

SEG
   3
      121: 30 n.47, 31 n. 53
   18
      36: 36 n.88
   24
      162: 36 n.88

Servius
      Aen. 6, 21: 36 n.85

SIG^2
      439: 50 n.138, 60 n.181
      587: 50 n.138

SIG^3
      921: ix n.5, 21 n.4, 24 n.12, 30
         n.48, 34 n.75, 38 n.99, 38
         n.102, 55 n.157, 60 n.182
      953: 39
      987: 50 n.140
      1021: 20 n.1

Solon
      F. 76 a (Ruschenbusch): 36
         n.89

Steph. Byz. = Stephanus Byzantinus *s.vv.*
    Δεκελεία: 45 n.119, 47 n.127
    πάτρα: i n.1

Suda *s.vv.*
    'Απατούρια: 38 n.96
    ἐλατήρ: 29 n.43
    θίασος: 57 n.163
    Κουρεῶτις: 29 n.40
    μειαγωγήσουσι: 26 n.24, 27
        nn.26 and 28
    μειαγωγία: 26 n.24, 27 nn.26
        and 28
    φράτερες: 31 n.58

Thucydides
  2
    16: 67 n.13

Timokles
    F. 9 (Kock): 36 n.88

Xenophon
  Hellenika
    7, 4, 4: 36 n.88

Zenobios
  II
    27: 50

INDEX OF SELECTED GREEK WORDS

'Αθηναῖοι: in state decrees: 30
αἴξ: φράτριος: 29 n.42
ἄλλοι: φράτερες: 58-59
ἀνάκρισις: 56-57, 69-71
ἀντίγραφον: 38, 38 n.98
ἅπαντες: φράτερες: 58-59, 73 n.21, 78-80
ἀπό: 41 n.107
ἀπογράφομαι: 59
ἀποδικάζω: 38-42, 38 nn.101-102, 62 n.3
ἀπόδικος: 39 n.103
ἀποθήκη: on Royal Estates: 3
ἀποψηφίζομαι: 38, 38 n.102, 42-43, 62 n.3,
    63-64, 66, 75

γραμματεῖον: 38, 38 nn.96-97, 60

δέ: 46 n.123
Δεκελειῆθεν: ἐκ δήμου: 46, 46 n.123, 48
    n.127; δημοτευόμενοι: 47, 47 nn.125
    and 127
Δεκελειόθεν: 45 n.119, 47, 47 n.127
Δεκελειεῖς: 35, 44-48, 45 n.119, 51
δῆμος: 30, 46, 46 nn.123-124
διαδικάζω: 33
διαδικασία: 33-36, 34 n.69, 57, 61-73, 78-
    79
διαψηφίζομαι: 34, 43
διαψήφισις: 34-35, 61, 63 n.4, 82
δίκη: 40-41, 41 n.106
δοκέω: in state and phratry decrees: 30-
    31, 42-43

εἰμί: εἶναι φράτερα: 42-43, 52-53
εἰσάγω: 37-38, 37 nn.93-95, 41, 52-53, 53
    n.149, 64-65; εἰσάγων, introducer:
    64-66, 64 n.7, 65 n.9
εἰσαγωγή: 68, 65, 68, 69, 71
ἐλατήρ: 29, 29 n.43
ἐξερημόω: 49
ἐπί: 43-44, 44 n.118
ἐπιψηφίζομαι: 43
ἔριφος: 29 n.42
εὔθυνα: 43
ἔφεσις: 34 n.69, 42, 42 n.109, 66, 75-85
ἐφίημι: 64, 66

ἡμίκραιρα: 27 n.29

θίασος: 57-58, 78, 79-80, 80 n.18

θιασῶται: 57, 71-73, 76, 78, 79-80, 82

ἱερεώσυνα: 25-30, 27 n.29
ἱερόν, τό: 38 n.97

κείρω: 29, 29 n.41
κούρειον: 28-30, 28 n.33, 29 n.33
κοῦρος: 28, 29 n.37
κωλήν: 27, 27 n.29

λογισταί: 43
λοιμός: 54
λοιπόν: 54, 62

Μεγάλη Βρύσις: "Great Spring": 1
μεῖον: 25-27, 27 n.26, 30
μείων: 26-27
μήπω: 35-36, 41

νόμος: 35-36, 70

ὅδε: archaism in decrees: 31; referring
    to passage following: 53 n.152
οἰκεῖοι: 79
οἰκία: 38 n.97, 50, 50 n.141; ἰδιωτική:
    50
οἶκος: 44-45, 48-52, 48, 48 nn.128 and 131,
    49, 49 nn.135-137, 50 n.141, 75-85;
    κοινός: 50
οἰνιστήρια: 30
ὄις: 27 n.28; φράτηρ: 29 n.42
οὗτος: 53

πάτρα: 48
πλευρόν: 27, 27 n.29
πόλεμος: 54
πόλις: 48
πρόβατον: 27 n.28
προσφοιτάω: 47
πρότερος: 59-60, 68, 68 n.14
πρῶτος: 59-60

στήλη: 20
συνηγορέω: 44
συνήγοροι: 43-44, 44 n.118, 52, 63, 81, 83-
    84

ὕστερος: 60

φέρω: 75, 79 n.15

φοιτάω: 51,
φράτερες: generic, in decrees: 30
φρατρίον: 60
φρατρίζω: 52-53, 52 n.150, 63, 63 n.5

ψηφίζομαι: 43
ψήφισμα: 56-57, 60, 68-69

GENERAL INDEX

Acharnai: road from Dekeleia to: 1
admission: to the phratry: viii, 26, 37-38, 37 nn.3-4, 38 n.95, 52-53; role of House of Dekeleians in: 81
adoption: 49
adulthood: 28
Aegina: 48
Aeolians: and phratries: vii
agora: of demes: 52 n.146
Aischines of Phegous: 55
altar: 20, 37, 37 n.92, 53; importance in phratry rites: 37; and oaths: 83-84
American School of Classical Studies in Athens: ix
Anarrusis: second day of Apatouria: 42
Anenkletos: son of Nikodemos of Dekeleia: 55
Anthesteria: vii
aorist: in decree of Hierokles: 36, 37, 41-42, 65-66; and the "extraordinary" scrutiny: 65-66; gnomic: 36 n.83
Apatouria: vii, 26, 42, 42 n.108, 54
Apollo: 52; Patroos: 20, 20 n.2
appeal: 42, 42 n.109, 71, 73, 75-85; and rejection: 64, 66; the role of the House of the Dekeleians in: 81
archon year: 31
Aristotle: Constitution of Athens as witness for phratry: vii n.1
Artemis: 29, 60
assessors: 43-44
Athena: Phratria: 20, 20 n.2, 37, 37 n.92
Atthidographers: as witnesses for phratry: vii, vii n.2
Attica: and phratries: vii

ballots: 31; taken from altar: 37, 37 n.90
barbershop: 46-47, 55
Binder, J.: x
boys: and koureion: 28; age at koureion: 28 n.32

Camp, J.: x
candidate: for introduction to phratry: 37, 64-65
celebrations of phratries: 21
children: introduction of: 56; age at meion: 26, 26 n.24, 61; and "regular" scrutiny: 68, 85; and "extraordinary" scrutiny: 65-66, 70
Chios: 50, 80
citizenship: and the phratry: vii, 33, 84-85; law of Perikles: 42, 54; amnesty

of 403: 42; of Plataians: 46
Constantine II, King of Greece: 3
Crete: 36

dating formulae: in phratry and state decrees: 31
debtor: defaulting: 33
decrees: of phratries: 56-57, 70
decree of Hierokles: 20, 32-55; description of physical text: 5; and stonemason: 22; and the "extraordinary" scrutiny: 33, 56, 61-68, 72-72; aorist in: 36
decree of Menexenos: 19-20, 59-60; description of physical text: 5; stonemason of: 23-24, 56
Decree of Nikodemos: 19-20, 39, 55-59; description of physical text: 5; stonemason of: 22; and the "regular" scrutiny: 33, 56, 61, 68-73; date of, relative to the decree of Hierokles: 55, 70, 70 n.16; formulaic opening: 56, 56 n.160
Dekeleia: 1, 22, 24, 32, 32 n.66, 33, 36, 37, 44-48, 53, 80-81; Dorians, Spartans and: 46, 55-56, 58; Dekeleian War: 54; cult of Leto at: 60
Dekeleians, demesmen: 45-48, 80-81; meeting place in city: 54-55
Dekeleians, House of: ix, 44-48, 45 n.119, 52, 75-85; "genos" of: 45, 47, 75; "phratry" of: 35, 45, 47, 75, 77, 82; identity of, and appeal: 42; involvement in "extraordinary" scrutiny: 84
Dekelos: 46
deme: affiliation and phratry: 24, 32, 84-85; meeting places of: 52, 52 n.146
Demeter: 52
Demetrius of Phaleron: as witness for phratry: vii n.1
Demotion son of Kydas: 36, 36 n.88; formation of name: 36
Demotionidai: ix, 32, 36, 37, 75-85; "genos" of: 35, 75, 77; phratry of: 36 n.84, 76-77; identity of, and appeal: 42, 75-85 and οἱ ἅπαντες φράτερες: 78-79
Demotionidai, "decrees of": as witness for Attic phratry: viii; bibliography of: viii-ix, 6; discovery of: 1; editions of: 1-3; description of stele: 5-6; organization and layout of: 19-20

Deutsches Archäologisches Institut: in Athens: x
Dikaiarchos: as witness for phratry: vii n.1
Dionysia: Greater: vii
Dionysos: Theater of: 60
diphthong, "false" or "spurious": 24, 28 n.33, 59
Dorians: and phratry: vii; and Dekeleia: 46
Dorpia: first day of Apatouria: 42, 54
Dyaleis: Attic phratry: 30-31, 31 n.55, 32

ear: part of perquisites: 27, 27 n.30, 29
editorial conventions: 7 n.1
Ekphantides son of Theodoros of Dekeleia: 25; lessee of mine: 25
erasures: in Decrees of the Demotionidai: viii, 11-12, 13-14, 22-25
erection of stele: 19, 21 formula: 25, 25 n.18; role of phratriarch: 32
Eukleides: archonship of: 54
Eupha[-]: patronymic of a priest: 22
Euphanes: 22
Euphantides of Dekeleia: father of Theodoros: 11-12, 22-25
Euphantides of Hal[-]: 24
Eutychides of Dekeleia: 45

family: names within: 23, 23 n.8; patriarchal character: 23, 23 n.10
fathers: introduce children to phratry: 26 n.24, 28, 61
fines: 20, 22, 32, 37, 54, 81-83; imposition by priest of the House of the Dekeleians: 81
flank: part of perquisites: 27, 29
Fulbright Foundation: ix

genos: 35, 50, 51, 56, 80, 84; patronymic form of names: 36; demotic form of names: 45
George I, King of Greece: 2
goat: sacrifice at koureion: 29
gods: of phratries: 20-21, 20 n.2, 52; and oaths: 83-84
Graces: 48
Graham, A.J.: ix
Great Spring: area at Tatoi: 1
Greek Archaeological Service: second Ephoria: x
Greek Ministry of Agriculture: x

Hagnias: 49
haunch: part of perquisites: 27, 29
heading: of inscription: 5, 19, 20-21
Helen: 46
Herakles: 30
Hermes: Ktenites: 29 n.38

Herms: area in Athens: 46-47, 54-55; "Stoa of": 55 n.156
hetairiai: 36-37
Hierokles: 21, 32-33
House, οἶκος: 48-52; of the Dekeleians: see Dekeleieis; of the Meliteans: see Melite; building: 48, 48 n.128, 49-52, 80-81; family: 48-49; and associations of seafarers from the Black Sea: 48, 48 n.128, 49; and deme meeting places: 51

Ikarieis: 45
inheritance: 33
inquiry, preliminary: in phratry scrutiny: 57
introduction: to phratry: 26, 26 n.2, 28, 37, 49, 56, 61; introducer: 37, 39, 64-65; candidate: 37; at Apatouria: 42
Ion: in the Atthidographers: vii n.2
Ionia: and phratry: vii; and Apatouria: 29 n.37, 42; loan words from: 29 n.37

Jameson, M.: ix
Julian Park Foundation: x

Kaufman, M.: ix
Kephisieis: 45
Kerykes: 49-50, 80
King of Greece: viii, x, 1-3
Kleisthenes: 32 n.66, 85; in the Atthidographers: vii n.2
Klytidai: 50
Könen, L.: x
Koureotis: name of: 28; third day of Apatouria: 26, 42
koureion: 25, 28-30, 60, 67; etymology of: 28-29; age of children at: 28 n.33; year following: 33; "in the year before" the: 59-60, 61-62, 66
Kydantidai: 36
Kydas: 36
Kydathenaion: 59

Lambert, S.: ix
Lampon of Aegina: 48
law: of the Demotionidai: 35-36, 56, 61, 70, 79; of phratries and hetairiai: 36; relation of phratry laws to those of Athens: 36, 61
lease: of mine: 25; of phratry property: 32
legitimacy: 61
Lellingos: caretaker of Royal Estate: x
Leto: 20, 60
Lewis, D.: ix

lexicographers: as witnesses for phratry: viii; and meion: 26, 26 n.22; and koureion: 28
liturgies: 33

McClellan, M.: x
meetings: of phratry: 31
meion: 25-27, 26 nn.22-25, 27 nn.26-28, 30, 67; etymology of: 26-27, 27 nn.26-27;
Melite: 50-51, 80; house of Meliteans: 50-51, 80
Menexenos: 59
metic: 46
Miller, S.: x
mine: lessee of: 25
Minos: 36
Mitsos, M.: x
molding, crowning: of inscription: 5
money: part of perquisites: 30
Museum of George I: 2-3; excavation of: 2; current state of: 3
Myrrinous: 32, 52

names: repetition within Greek families: 23, 23 n.8
Nikodemos of Dekeleia: 32, 55-56; family of: 55-56; grave plot of: 56
notices: of phratry, posted by phratriarch: 32, 68

oaths: 20, 22, 32, 37, 43, 52, 69, 83-84
Ober, J.: ix
Oion Dekeleikon: 32, 32 nn.64 and 66
Oion Kerameikon: 32
Ostwald, M.: ix
orators: Attic, as witnesses for phratry: vii-viii

Palmer, R.E.A.: ix
Pankleon of Plataia: 46-47
pankration: victor in: 48
Pantakles of Oion: 32, 32 n.64
patronymic: form of phratry and genos names: 36
Peloponnesian War: 46, 54, 85
Peppas-Delmousou, D.: x
Peradotto, J.: ix
Perikles: citizenship law of: 42, 54
perquisites of priest: 19, 21, 25-30; physical description of text: 5;
Phanias of Dekeleia: 55
Phanodemos son of Nikodemos of Dekeleia: 55
Phegous: 55
Philoumene, mother of Theodoros: 55
Philoumene, daughter of Theodoros: 55
phratriarch: 31-32, 31 n.58; and priest: 22, 22 n.2, 32, 83-84; number of: 31,

31 n.55, 32; annual term: 31; "phratriarch year": 31, 31 n.57; presides at phratry meetings: 31; and voting procedure: 31, 53, 63; fines imposed on: 82
Phormion: archon at Athens: 31
phratry: vii-viii; among Ionians: vii; among Dorians and Aeolians: vii; in Attica: vii; evidence for: vii-viii; and males: vii; and females: vii; and citizenship: vii; role in Attic festivals: vii; internal organization: viii; seniority within: 23, 23 n.10; geographic character: 24, 32, 45, 84-85; patronymic form of names: 36; membership: 52-53; fragmentation of pre-Kleisthenic phratries: 76, 76 n.5
Phylakidas son of Lampon of Aegina: 48
Plataia: battle of: 45; and Dekeleia: 46-47; Pankleon of: 46-47
polemarch: 46
preamble: of inscription: 19, 30-32; state formulae: 30
priest: of phratry: 21-22; erasure of names of: 11-12, 21-25, 55; and perquisites: 25-30; and phratriarch: 22, 22 n.2, 32; of House of Dekeleians: 81-83; nomenclature of: 83
priesthood: gentilitial: 23, 23 n.9; held for life: 23, 23 n.8; succession: 22-25
property: of phratry: 32; division of: 33
prosecutors: 43-44, 44 n.117
Psalychiadai: 48
publication of inscription: 19-20, 22, formula: 25, 25 n.18
Pyanopsion: 42
Pyrgos: Museum on royal estate: 2

register: of phratries: 22, 32; of Demotionidai: 38, 38 nn.96-97, 61; copy of: 38, 38 n.98; of demes, revision: 34, 61 priest, phratriarch and: 38, 38 n.100
regulations of phratries: 22
rejection: of a candidate: 38-42, 38 n.102, 43
rent: on phratry property: 32
rites of passage: vii, 28, 29 and shearing: 29
Royal Estates: viii, x, 1-3; devastated by fire: 2

sacrifices: 20, 25-30, 54
Salaminioi: 45
sanctuaries: and phratries: 22 and phratry register: 38

Sannios of Dekeleia: 25
Sannios son of Stratokles of Dekeleia: 25
Santirocco, M.: x
Schmidt, G.: x
scholiasts: as witnesses for phratry: viii; and meion: 26, 26 n.22; and koureion: 28
scrutiny: 33-36, 61-73
scrutiny, "extraordinary": ix, 33-36, 41, 43, 45, 53, 54, 56, 61-68, 72-73, 78; and children: 65-66, 70; time of: 33; organization of: 61-68; digressions, in: 62-68; and House of Dekeleians: 84; and deme διαψήφισις: 34-35; circumstances leading to: 66-67; fines imposed in: 81-83; compared to "regular": 72-73, 78
scrutiny, "regular": ix, 33-36, 41, 56, 61, 68-73, 78; and children: 68; avoidance of: 41-42; fines in: 81-83; compared to extraordinary: 72-73, 78
shearing: sheep: 29, 29 n.38; and koureion: 29
sheep: sacrifice at meion: 27; sacrifice at koureion: 29
Solon: in the Atthidographers: vii n.2; and the laws of phratries: 36-37
Sophanes son of Eutychides of Dekeleia: 45
Sparta: and Dekeleia: 46, 54, 58
Stavrides: manager of Royal Estates in Greece: x, 3
stele: 5-6, 20; erection of: 19, 21, 25; average proportions in Attica: 53 n.153
Stoa of the Herms: 55 n.156
Stoa of the King: 55
Stoa Poikile: 55
stoichedon: viii, 5-6, 11-14, 23-24, 53, 55, 59
stonemason: 11-12, 22, 23
Stratokles of Dekeleia: 25
subdivisions of phratries: 57-59, 78-80; and οἱ ἄλλοι φράτερες: 79-80, 79 n.16
Synoikia: vii

Tatoi: viii, x, 1-3
Thargelia: vii
Theater of Dionysos: 60
Thebes of Mykale: 29 n.38
Theodoros of Dekeleia: 25
Theodoros son of Euphantides of Dekeleia: 11-12, 22-25, 59; deme affiliation: 24, 32; family of: 24-25
Theodoros son of Stratokles of Dekeleia: 25
Therrikleidai: Attic phratry: 20 n.2

Theseus: 36, 46, 46 n.124
Themistios of Aegina: 48
thiasos: religious association: 57; subdivision of phratry: 57-58
Thymaitis: Attic phratry: 20 n.2
trierarch: 24
trittys: 32 n.66
twelve kingdoms: of Attica: 32 n.66
Tyndaridai: 46

Vanderpool, E.: x
voting: of phratry: 31, 36, 42-43, 71-72

wine: part of perquisites: 29-30
witnesses: 68 swear holding to altar: 37 and thiasoi: 58

Zeus: 52; Phratrios: 20, 20 n.2, 24, 37, 37 n.92, 52, 70-71

Ill. 1: Face A (Photo DAI Athen, neg. no. 83/579).

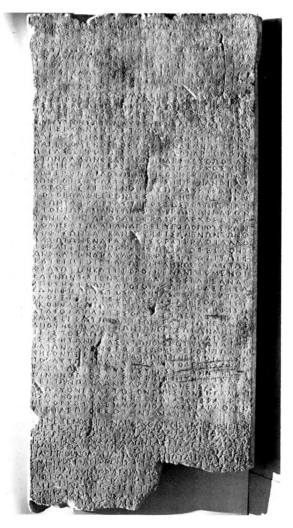

Ill. 2: Face B (Photo DAI Athen, neg. no. 83/582).

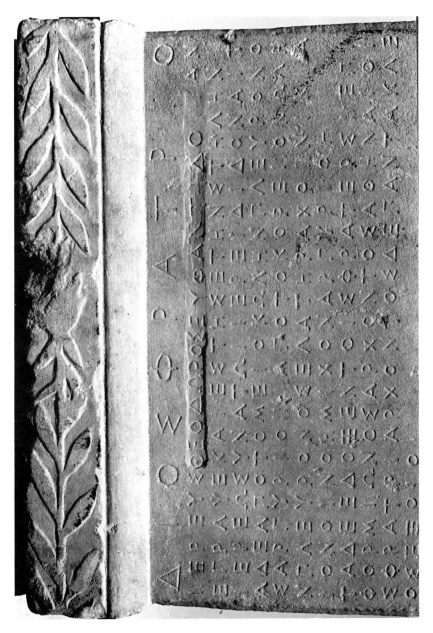

Ill. 3: Detail of Face A, lines 1-12 (Photo DAI Athen, neg. no. 83/580).

Ill. 4: Detail of Face A, lines 38-57 (Photo DAI Athen, neg. no. 83/581).

Ill. 5: Detail of Face B, lines 59-81 (Photo DAI Athen, neg. no. 83/583).

Ill. 6: Detail of Face B, lines 105-126 (Photo DAI Athen, neg. no. 83/584).